What I've Learned About Bigfoot:

50 Years and Counting

By

Mary M. Fabian

12/2022

Cover Art by Angel 'Xander' Thomas

DEDICATION

This book is dedicated, Firstly, to my Lord and Savior, my Best Friend and confidant, Jesus Christ.

My Husband, my Love, my Rock, my Sounding Board and Devils Advocate, Louis Fabian.

My Sister, always at my and by my side, whom I continually torture and torment until the end of time, Deborah Kaye Parker-McGee

My Daughter, of whom I am so Proud of for her achievements, even though she's a Skeptic, Melanie Barton-Sperduto

My granddaughter, Angel Thomas, for her cover art that I tweaked by adding the 'figure' by the tree.

All of my Grandchildren and Future Great Grandchildren

My Mentor, Tim "Coonbo" Baker. Thank you so very much for Sharing your Knowledge & Wisdom!

The Bigfoot Outlaws, for your Knowledge and willingness to teach and Share!

Brian Seech and Fred Saluga, the same. Thank you so very much for being there and sharing your knowledge!

Bill Rigby for being such a loyal Teammate and Good Friend!

My Pennsylvania Bigfoot Project Research Team, ever changing, shrinking and growing over the years, and all Great Friends!

My Pennsylvania Bigfoot Project Leads of all levels, Administrators & Moderators.

My Pennsylvania Bigfoot Project Group Members, at this time, 17,400+ and growing!

My Friends, too numerous, and I don't want to insult anyone by forgetting a name!

I wrote this because everyone kept bugging me that I need to write this. And so I did. And it's been burning in me to get it down on paper, organized and, I hope, complete. I've written various articles for various magazines, papers and blogs, and have included those pertaining to Bigfoot here. I've also written short stories, one published, and have a fictional novel waiting to get down on paper.

Misspellings, grammar mistakes are all on me. Some content was copied directly from Journals and Logbooks.

If I forgot anything, along with Future Encounters and Sightings will be for Future Editions of this Book. I do hope there are more! I'm still learning about these amazing creatures.

Mary M. Fabian

December 28, 2022

TABLE OF CONTENTS

DEDICATION

CHAPTER 1: THE MAGICIANS DAUGHTER

CHAPTER 2: THE GHOST

CHAPTER 3: MY FIRST BIGFOOT SIGHTING - THE WILD MAN

CHAPTER 4: FORT NECESSITY

CHAPTER 5: THE 'TWEEN YEARS

CHAPTER 6: MY SECOND BIGFOOT SIGHTING

CHAPTER 7: TAG! YOU'RE IT!

CHAPTER 8: NIGHT OF TERROR

CHAPTER 9: WHOOPS!

CHAPTER 10: BLOBSQUATCH

CHAPTER 11: PENNSYLVANIA BIGFOOT PROJECT

CHAPTER 12: MY THIRD BIGFOOT SIGHTING

CHAPTER 13: HABITUATION

CHAPTER 14: MY FOURTH BIGFOOT SIGHTING

CHAPTER 15: ZAPPED

CHAPTER 16: MY FIFTH BIGFOOT SIGHTING

CHAPTER 17: EMF, BIGFOOT, TRAIL & GAME CAMERAS

CHAPTER 18: THERE BE BIGFOOT

CHAPTER 19: 10 COMMANDMENTS OF BIGFOOTING

CHAPTER 20: VARIOUS THOUGHTS

CHAPTER 21: SINEAD'S ENCOUNTER

CHAPTER 22: LOGBOOK

END THOUGHTS

PHOTOS

Chapter 1 The Magicians Daughter

I stood perfectly still as my Dad wound a rope around me. Round and round, tightly woven. He stood back and ordered me to escape from it. Which I did. Easily. I was 5 years old. My Dad was a Magician, "Parker the Magician", performing at small stage shows in the Western Pennsylvania area. He told me that he would usually pick the biggest, strongest looking man in the audience, give him the rope and tell him to tie up his assistant on the stage. Joyfully, the man usually would. Very tightly and thoroughly.

Now, I had never performed on stage with my Dad. He had performed this trick with his first wife or and his first daughter, my half sister, Dorothy, as his stage assistant.

But I knew how to escape from that rope trick just in case my Dad ever wanted to perform it again. Most shows at that time were held at church basements, VFW's and later on, at nursing homes. He taught me other tricks, how to 'magically' be glued to the ground when a big strong man would try to pick me up.

He tried to teach me other tricks, to pass on his act to me, but I honestly wasn't interested. I still have most of his magic paraphernalia on display in my home, some with my daughter, Melanie. It'll all get passed on down to my grandkids. Maybe one day one of them will show interest.

TBT - My dad, Roy E. Parker aka Parker the Magician See More

Caption

The most important thing that I learned that has been useful throughout my life, is learning how to spot that most important Magicians trick, 'Misdirection' and using Illusions to fool people. But, about that later …..

My Dad never played Vaudeville or the 'Big Time'. Magic was the gravy when he worked his full time job as an electrician at the various steel mills around the country, as well as being his Bread and Butter during the Depression. Church basements, Fire Halls, VFW's, birthday parties were always there. And during the hard times, a small time magician didn't ask for a lot of money to play a small venue. You got what you were given and was happy with it.

In 1937 he joined the International Brotherhood of Magicians.

My Dad used his first wife and his daughter, my half sister, Dorothy, in his act during those days, up into the 40's until they divorced. Then Dorothy became his full time assistant.

He re-married in 1951 to my mother, Helen Knight. My sister, Debbie, was born in '53, I was born in '55. We lived in a small town, Vanderbilt, in Fayette County in SWPA. This is where my Dad practiced the rope trick with me. I remember standing on the back porch of our home on Walnut Street, with him practicing with me.

Now, I was a daredevil, even then. I'd climb to the very top of the tree in our yard, to the high thin top where it was nice

Myself and my son, Michael playing with
a Monkey 1980

and flexible. It was the greatest fun, I remember, to sway the
tree top back and forth and round and round, hanging on and
laughing. If I saw a tree, I'd scramble right up. My Dad had
a few nicknames for me, but during those times it was 'Little
Monkey'.

Our Gramma Parker lived with us, in her little Mother-in-
Law apartment on the back of the house. I'd go down every
morning and eat breakfast with her. Shredded Wheat with
chocolate milk on it. She'd have her Shredded Wheat with
coffee poured over. She was a strong, tiny woman of deep
Faith. Every morning, she'd have her Bible out, reading it at
the table. She'd tell me 'Pray Everyday'. I took that to
heart, and I still do.

My Dad's full time job was as an Electrician at US Steel Clairton Works in Clairton, PA. That was a 20 mile, one way, commute for him. After Gramma Parker died, he decided to move closer to his job. So, we moved from our wonderful big home next to the Vanderbilt Church of Christ, in the small town of Vanderbilt where even at age 5 I could walk to the store and buy myself a bag of m&m's and a bottle of YooHoo chocolate pop, sit in the booth with my 5 year old 'boyfriend', Dale, and drink our YooHoo's.

We moved to Clairton PA. A classic Steel Mill Town. I hated it. The kids in my elementary school made fun of me. A skinny kid with an overbite who didn't play mean games like they did. I was the butt of the joke. I became a loner, always exploring the nearby park by myself or with my sister, Debbie. I'd haunt the school library and the town Library, reading Zane Grey and Edgar Rice Burroughs.

HEY! You said this book was about the Wild Man! BIGFOOT! Get to it!

Ok, OK! Be patient ......

My Dad always told me 'Patience is a virtue.' I took that to heart, also, along with to Pray Everyday.

In Spring,1967, we moved to a 100 acre farm in Jefferson Borough, a different school district. We had horses, sheep, ducks, one rooster, a dog and cat. I was in my glory there. Fresh air. Helping my Dad in the barn or the garden. Taking walks in the apple orchard with him telling me stories, and teaching me how to walk silently. How to be still out in the open and no one notice you, as if you were invisible. He told me about the Wild Man during those days. I honestly don't recall specifically what he told me, perhaps when he was a child, his Dad may have told him about the Wild Man in Fayette County.

What is the Wild Man, you ask? During those days, Bigfoot was known as the 'Wild Man'. People sometimes thought Bigfoot was a feral human, or a hermit. But the impression I had gotten from my Dad was that the Wild Man was something different from a human. Or part human. We honestly, and regretfully, didn't talk very much about this subject. He was always teaching me different things, and that was only very lightly touched on. Perhaps he didn't know very much. I wish now that I could share all of this with him. He'd have been right there with me all along this journey.

Chapter 2 The Ghost

I explored our new home, the farm, and beyond. We had a huge bank barn that was so much fun to play in. I'd climb to the highest rafters and run along them, jumping from one beam to the other. We'd catch the big black snakes that would come up into the yard by the house and carry them down to the barn where they'd find more food and be of use taking care of the mice and other critters. He'd always slither back up to the front yard, and we'd carry him back down to the barn. One day, we found him smashed flat where one of the horses stomped him.

Our home was an old farmhouse, over 100 years old at that time in the 60's. At some point in time before we moved in, a bathroom was installed in the hallway from the back hall to the back porch, off of the stairway to the bedrooms. Every so often, when my sister and I would be up late on Saturday night watching Bill Cardille and Chiller Theater, we'd hear footsteps walking down the stairs, and into the bathroom. For the longest time, we just assumed it was one of our parents going to the bathroom in the middle of the night. It wasn't, we later found out.

One Sunday morning, we asked our Mom & Dad if it was one of them who came down at night, since we called out, but no one answered. They both replied, 'Neither of us came down last night.' Perplexed, my sister and I looked at one another. We told our Dad about hearing the footsteps walking down the stairs late at night. He had a strange look on his face, but said nothing. Years later, he shared told us about the ghost of the old woman who used to live in the farmhouse, how he watched her walking down the stairs one night, past him, turn and walk into the bathroom. During her time, the bathroom wasn't there, but was a hallway with a door to the back porch.

Another night, when I was a few years older, I was laying in bed, about ready to fall asleep. I heard footsteps walking up the stairs. I knew my Dad and Mom were in their bedroom across the hallway. My sister was in her bedroom, moved downstairs off that back hallway when she turned 13. I was alone. I listened to the footsteps make the turn to the next landing, then up to our floor. I heard her walking and turn towards my bedroom, walking in and towards my bed! I prayed 'Dear Jesus! Take it away! Don't let it get me!' I pulled the blankets up over my head and tried to pretend I was asleep. She/It walked next to my bed at the head of the bed, and stopped. I lay there quaking in fear, shaking but doing my best to stay quiet and still. I heard her finger tapping, as if in impatience on the nightstand next to my bed.

TAP TAP TAP TAP TAP!

Quiet. I listened hard.

Quiet. Nothing. I prayed hard, and fell asleep eventually. That was the last time I heard her. God answered my Prayer! Thank You, Lord!

Chapter 3 The Wild Man

Summer of 1967, learning roaming about the farm and nearby woods, I explored. The pine grove, the apple orchard, the forest at the top, the valley at the bottomland the field across from the house, and the gas line. Later on, I'll relate something else I discovered about that gas line. The gas line at the back of our farm begged to be followed. I walked up to the gas line and turned left toward Beam Run Road. Down the steep hill to the road and across, up the hill and over. On that downslope into a dip before going uphill again, there was a thick wooded area on my right and an overgrown field on my left.

I started downslope towards the dip. My eyes were drawn to the movement of a figure walking out of the woods to my right across from me. He stopped in the middle of the gas line, almost directly across from me on the upslope. It was a very large, bulky, 'Man'. He had a 'husky' build, bulky, big and tall. Messy black hair on his head and face, which I took, at that distance, to be a beard. He seemed to be wearing a matching black fur coat, which I found to be very strange since it was summertime.

His face resembled the Neanderthals on the movie 'One Million Years B.C.' that we had seen at the theater the year before.

He looked at me, very mild, no emotion showing on his face, turned and continued on, into the overgrown field across.

Very brief. The entire encounter only lasted maybe 10 seconds total.

I thought he was a Man. A big hairy Neanderthal Man wearing a fur coat.

That memory stuck with me for 50 years until it clicked and I realized what I saw and why the memory of that encounter stuck with me.

I honestly couldn't tell you how tall he was, or any specific features. I was 11 years old, and all I could compare him to was the Neanderthal guy in the movie from the previous year.

I wish I could. But, the distance of about 50 yards and the years between have faded that memory.

But the point of the matter is, I remembered a very brief, innocuous encounter with a stranger over 50 years later. And was able to connect the dots of what exactly I saw.

Skipping ahead 50 years, yes, the realization floored me. At that time, I was in denial that I had ever seen a Bigfoot. Yes, he was a Bigfoot. And he was my First Sighting.

I don't think that he followed me home, but knowing Bigfoot behavior as I know now, he likely knew where I lived. But he never came, and I never saw another while living on the farm, as much, as deep, and far that I explored.

Chapter 4 Fort Necessity

My Dad retired from the steel mill in 1970. He had a Ford pickup truck with a cap on the back that he fixed up to sleep inside. It was too small for the family of 4, so he bought a truck camper.

We camped at Cook Forest Campground, in the Allegheny National Forest. First thing in the morning, after breakfast, I'd run outside and disappear into the forest to explore. I'd find fascinating game trails to follow with fascinating features like boulders to climb on and tall trees to climb.

One night, my Dad woke us up and told us to look out the window. There was a black bear wandering around the campground, raiding coolers. He walked towards our truck and disappeared underneath. Suddenly, our camper started rocking back and forth! The bear was scratching his back on the undercarriage of the truck!

After that, my Dad bought a 21' long trailer to camp in. That was luxury!

After that, we mostly camped at Fort Necessity campground in the Laurel Highlands off of route 40 in Farmington PA. But you say, 'There's NO campground at Fort Necessity!' There was then. And it was FREE. Now, the old campground area is the picnic area with old rotting shelters and abandoned, rusty fountains.

Like at Cook Forest, first thing after breakfast, I'd run off into the forest and explore. I'd be gone all day, only finding my way back to the camper at suppertime. It was a nice, friendly community at that campground. Mostly filled with retirees and their motorhomes. A British family stayed for one weekend in their RV. They were traveling & exploring the US for the summer. I made friends with the daughter, who was about my age. We played badminton all weekend. Wish I could remember their names, but that's been too long ago.

Yes, my sister, Debbie, came along on our camping trips. She and I would occasionally walk down the path to the Fort where we would play cowboys and Indians. We'd take turns on who would win and who would lose. I didn't like to lose. So, no matter what, I mostly won those 'battles'. She wouldn't hike with me, though. I think she stayed mostly in the trailer, reading her 'Tiger Beat' magazines and mooning over The Beatles.

I was outdoors, in the mountains and fresh air. Hiking in the woods, practicing walking silently as an Indian and being invisible. I was in absolute Heaven! My imagination took me on many adventures out in that forest!

I'd find the best paths into the deepest hollows. I'd find these trees interwoven into elaborate structures. I'd look at them in wonder. Even then, as a kid, I could tell that they weren't caused by a storm, wind, snow, or rot. They were dragged into that place, fresh green trees and braided into one another. I'd hike on after studying them along the trail, only to get pelted by rocks. I wondered who was throwing rocks at me and why? But, when that would happen, and it happened a few times as I was hiking back there, I would look in the direction of the thrower and tell them, 'Ok, I'm turning around and going away.' And I would go in another direction. I never saw a figure or heard any vocals. I'd just get pelted with rocks.

Chapter 5 The 'Tween Years 1972 to 2004

In 1972, I was 16 years old, and pregnant, and so, I got married.

We lived in a small village where the neighbors were clannish and unfriendly. I had 2 children. There wasn't much outdoors or forest discovery then. It was Life as a Housewife, Mother, college student and part time jobs Jill of All Trades in a Suburb of Pittsburgh PA.

In 2000 we divorced. And I rediscovered the Forest. And my Peace.

I hiked various trails and forests in Western Pennsylvania, the Laurel Highlands, hiked and cross country skied the mountains in Quebec and Ontario. Hiked the mountains above Colorado Springs, in Colorado.

I played tennis, worked out, exercised, and worked 100+ hours a week at my job.

I scrambled to move up the 'corporate ladder' at my insurance job, and tried not to go insane or have a stroke.

I also attended conventions dedicated to fans of the author, Edgar Rice Burroughs, participated in discussion boards on various subjects, and was the model for an artist drawing an ERB heroine, Dian The Beautiful, for a magazine.

My life as a single woman was busy. I tried to stay busy and occupied. I met and dated quite a few very nice guys, was proposed to many times, got engaged, but I knew I hadn't met the Right One yet.

Until early 2004, and Lou.

Chapter 6 My Second Bigfoot Sighting

My Bigfoot "Family"

The SOB - Beaver County PA 2004 to 2016

I met and married Lou in 2004. God Blessed us both. And no, Lou isn't the SOB.

Read on, that's to come …..

I moved to Lou's home in northern Beaver County, PA. North Sewickley Township. Almost immediately, the Bigfoot activity started. Perhaps it was going on all along at Lou's home, just that he never noticed it. He had purchased his home from the estate of an elderly couple. I've a feeling that either the wife or husband knew the Bigfoot were there, and were coming around, and were even perhaps feeding them. Which is a Huge No-No. Later in this book, I'll attach my article on the practice of "Habituation by 'Gifting' With Food".

I would wake up in the middle of the night to either a BANG on the side of the house directly behind my head while I was asleep in bed, or to a gravelly-growly deep voice, which I now know to be called 'Samurai Chatter'. Now, having previously lived in a couple 'Haunted' houses, my first thought was that this was the ghost of the previous owner, perhaps the elderly gentleman was angry at me for something. But that didn't jive, since all that I had heard about him was that he was a very friendly handicapped man who would sit on the front porch in good weather and wave at everyone who would pass by on the road in front of the house. I prayed about it and him, that he would find rest and not bother me.

Well, that didn't work.

As the years went by, and the Bigfoot that I nicknamed 'The SOB' would pull other tricks, I learned that he was on a routine. He would come by almost every 2 1/2 to 3 weeks. He'd turn the motion sensor light on the back porch so that it wouldn't trigger. He'd come in close to the door where my Border Collie would lay every day and evening on watchful alert on the inside.

She'd react and alert me that he was there. Her hackles would raise, she'd give a mixture of a soft growl and whine. She would crawl, backwards, away from the door, eyes fixed on the door, until she was huddled up against me, shaking in terror. This went on until we moved in 2016. I would hear vocals late at night, sounds I couldn't identify. I would explore online databases to see what kind of creature would make those sounds. I heard him give a loud WHOOOO-OOOOP! WHOOOO-OOOOP! WHOOOO-OOOOP! from just on the other side of the stone wall behind my home. I'd hear a distant call/whistle, low pitch to high every few years, very late at night. I found a YouTube channel, Lord Cryptid, where both vocals matched what he had recorded and called 'Sasquatch'.

BIGFOOT! They are actually in Pennsylvania?!? I discovered that yes, they are here. And I had one harassing me and my dog at my home in Beaver County PA!

I remembered what I had seen as a child, that memory of that Hairy Man that stuck in the back of my memory all of these years.

I had no other name for him, other than the Hairy Man. What I had seen as a child in Jefferson Borough, Allegheny County PA was actually a Bigfoot!

That was a revelation to me.

And here, I was encountering another one. And he was a real SOB. A Bully. Harassing me, and terrifying my dear Zhina.

I would go outside into the back yard on sunny days to dry my hair. One day, I was sitting out there, whistling and singing while drying my hair, when I saw him. He raised his head and was looking at me from over the top of the stone wall. The sun was behind him, silhouetting

Photo of Zhina at Her Post by the Back Door - Ever Watchful for the SOB

him, so that I couldn't make out his features. His hair was gorgeous. It gave off a glinting and sparkling reddish gold. I looked right at him and told him 'I SEE YOU, YOU SOB!' He ducked his head behind the wall and must've crawled away. I don't recall if he banged on the wall or scared my dog that night, or not.

Around this timeframe, there was a tv show on about a crew of people going around the country searching for Bigfoot. They'd bang on the trees and do these howls. For fun one afternoon, while the grandkids were visiting, I got a sturdy tree limb, and we banged on a tree and howled. We shut up and listened. From the woods across the road, from about 500 yards away, deep in those woods, I heard a single knock. That startled me. I only half believed that this is what they were.

This among other things convinced me that the Bigfoot is what I was dealing with.

I had purchased a Bigfoot statue and another statue of a Wizard and on of an Ent (Lord of the Rings). I had them in the front of the yard by the road. People used to stop and take pictures of the Bigfoot statue because we had it set up as if he was real and walking through a boulder field and forest. I used to watch the birds how they would react to that and the other statues. The birds would swoop and 'dive bomb' the Bigfoot statue, but they would ignore the Wizard and Ent statue. That was thought provoking.

I'd holler at my husband and ask him why he kept turning the motion sensor light at the back of the house, so it wouldn't trigger. He denied turning it. We lived in a 1950's low ranch home. There was a church across the road and a country club. Behind us was undeveloped property and another golf course. A little over a mile away is Ellwood City, a small city in Lawrence County. Famous for Donnie Iris and the movie 'Bigfoot: The Movie'.

The Connoquennessing Creek runs in the valley below that house. The creek runs eventually, into the Beaver River, a mile or so on the other side of the hill from us. It's rural, forested area, deep river valleys, old coal mines and railroad tracks. There is also a power line cut up the hill.

One day, after watching the tv show about Bigfoot, I decided to imitate them calling a Bigfoot. I had an errand to run on the other side of the hill, so I took a short cut, and took the road behind my house, up over the hill and into the deeper part of the forest. I stopped in the middle of the road, opened the door, cupped my hands around my mouth and let out a couple of Whoops. I stopped and listened. Silence. Not even birdsong. I shrugged my shoulders and drove the mile back home at the bottom of the hill.

I was learning the SOB's habits and some motivations.

I'd go outside to the back yard after showering, to dry my hair in the sunshine. I'd sit back there, or work in my garden, singing a song, or just read a book.

I can't remember what exactly I was doing, if I was just sitting in the sunshine, or what, but I recall that I saw movement at the top of the stone wall bordering our backyard. It was evening, the sun was starting to set. I saw a large hairy head looking over the wall at me, silhouetted by the setting sun. I knew immediately who and what it was. I looked right at him, pointed my finger and wagged my finger at him. I said 'I see you, you SOB!'. He quickly ducked his head down and I didn't see anymore of him.

What I did see during that short period of time was just the silhouette of his head, which I could tell was hair covered. He had long reddish gold hair that sparkled in the setting sunshine. Unfortunately, I couldn't make out any features. He was about 30 yards away.

Over the years, I had attempted to find others around me, any neighbors, who were also experiencing what I was, without success. And so, in 2015, on Facebook, I began Pennsylvania Bigfoot Project, my organization. Over the intervening years, I had dug and searched, trying to find answers to questions. I spoke with and wrote many different Bigfoot Researchers all over the United States. I could not find anyone who shared Common Sense, logical answers to my questions about this creature. Until I met The Bigfoot Outlaws, Tim "Coonbo" Baker, Jim "Bubba Gump" Hart, and Jim "Bear" King. These men were out of Alabama and Mississippi, had grown up with Bigfoot, or 'Boogers' as they called them, on their properties. These men had decades of experience and knowledge gleaned from experiments based on what "Coonbo" had learned as a NASA Scientist, working with infrasound on the NASA Shuttles and military complex. "Coonbo" and "Bubba Gump" call themselves "High Tech Rednecks".

Jim "Bubba Gump" Hart passed away in 2022, but his legacy, humor, and knowledge live on in we who loved him for what he was.

They spoke Common Sense language to questions. 'Think like a Booger.' Was their advice. And yes, that helps very very much, as to learning their motivations.

Food, Water, and Shelter. The Three Necessities of Life.

I met the Outlaws in person at their Meet & Greet in 2017 at their camp at Land Between the Lakes, Kentucky. That week was an adventure, especially if you've heard the stories about LBL and the Dog Man. We heard vocals, saw eyeshine, saw shadows creeping up on our camp. One person found the body of a coyote killed by a Bigfoot. Twisted and wrung like an old dish towel.

I'd campout at Salt Fork State Park in Cambridge Ohio, up in the Allegheny National Forest, in the Forbes State Forest, and various dispersed campsites in Western PA and Ohio.

I had fixed up my pickup truck with a cap/topper, with a raised bed inside. Memory foam mattress, curtains and a 'luggable loo' completed my camping shelter.

My truck has been shaken with me sleeping inside a couple of times. I've had tree limbs and rocks thrown at me. I've been growled at, and seen 5 Bigfoot so far.

Chapter 7 'Tag! You're it!'

The Theory of Bigfoot Somehow 'Tagging' People

Many Hours of hiking miles in the mountains, of Pennsylvania, Quebec, Ontario, and Colorado, I saw no Bigfoot sign. I was less experienced then. I had seen the one when I was a child. I had seen the tree structures when I was a child. I would have recognized similar if I would have seen it, but I didn't.

But, and I have heard this from others who have had multiple sightings and encounters, that in some way, they can 'Tag' you. Perhaps on a cellular level with EMF? Who knows?

After digging quite a bit, I found an article that may possibly support that theory.

From "Biological effects of non-ionizing electromagnetic fields: Two sides of a coin" by authors Timur Saliev, Dinara Begimbetova, Abdul-RazakMasoud, and Bakhyt Matkarimov

"The results showed a significant increase in DNA strand breaks in the cells exposed to extremely low-frequency EMF. At the same time, the researchers reported that the exposure to radiofrequency EMF led to significant increase of oxidative DNA base damage (SAR 4 W/kg)."

https://www.sciencedirect.com/science/article/pii/S00796107183O1007

It's a fascinating article, and I highly recommend you, the Reader, to look it up and read it.

So, it is possible to be 'Tagged' on a cellular level by low levels of EMF. Do the Bigfoot do that? I don't know. It's entirely possible. Both animals and humans can emit low levels of EMF and radiation. Animals can sense EMF. Deer will avoid trail cams because they may be able to sense the EMF radiating from the electronics.

Chapter 8 "Night of Terror"

As a mom, I had to be a light sleeper, to stay alert to teenage antics. So, after a few months, I found myself waking up to a sudden bang on the wall behind my side of the bed. One single hard bang. That's it. Or I'd awaken to mumbling, garbled speech.

I'd put the banging to deer hitting their antlers against the house. Or a ghost of the former owner. Same with the speech. I thought it was a ghost.

Even though I had a previous Bigfoot sighting, that had been when I was a kid, and not something I dwelled on, so I didn't make the connection immediately.

I moved to North Sewickley Twp in 2004 when I re-married. A year later, we got a Border Collie, a rescue. A beautiful timid girl who never barked. Through alot of love and positive human interaction, we helped regain her confidence and voice. What happened with her and the Bigfoot is another story.

I'd take the occasional walk up an old game trail behind my home to a hill behind us, owned by the golf course. Up top was a very scenic view of the valley, and so worth the hike up the steep track. One afternoon, I was going to head up the animal trail, when I discovered a huge tree branch blocking it. There were trees next to the trail, but strangely enough, somehow, this branch didn't come from any of those trees. It was a mystery, but I didn't wonder about it. It was just there, and I had to climb over it on an uphill slant. It made the trek more complicated, but it was still worth it.

Someone mentioned a tv show to me after my Bigfoot statue was stolen, about Bigfoot aka "Not Finding

Bigfoot", so I watched it. I imitated the tree knocks in my back yard for fun with my grandkids. I even heard a single knock in reply from the woods across the street. I thought, oh that's just neighborhood kids! Then, I thought, well, maybe it is a Bigfoot around here, maybe I should imitate the guys on the tv show and do some whoops! So, I drove up top of the hill, opened the car window in a remote area, and let out a couple whoops. And listened ..... nothing. Oh well! Nothing around here! Later, that same night, I woke up at 2am with banging on the wall behind the bed. Multiple bangs. Then bangs on the roof. More bangs on the wall behind the bed. It was terrifying! What was happening??!!?? Who was doing that??

This went on for almost a half hour!

My husband slept thru them, until I finally woke him up. He was still half asleep and not very alert. He thought I was imagining it. There is no plumbing or HVAC in that wall, or above us. We had motion sensor lights all around the house, but somehow, that side of the house got missed when he installed the lights.

That was the only night when there were multiple bangs. After that, it went back to just an occasional bang. But every 3 weeks, we had a visitor who would slip up behind the motion sensor light, peek into our patio door (which had the interior blinds), and torment our dog for a few minutes before moving on.

So, doing tree knocks & whoops, when you are close to home, and you don't know what the signals mean, or what the different whoops & vocals mean, you're only asking for trouble.

If you can't speak their language, don't try to imitate it.

Chapter 9 Whoops!

One weekend evening, I was getting ready for bed. It was about 12:30 at night. We had moved the bed so that the headboard was on the wall at the front of the house. Well lit, that SOB wasn't going to hit the wall behind my head anymore! My side of the bed was on the wall that he would come around and hit. I had a nice slider window that I kept cracked open for a fresh breeze. My husband would be huddled under 10 heavy quilts, and I'd be there with only the sheet, welcoming that breeze, year 'round.

Getting changed into my nightgown, I heard a noise outside.

Whooo-ooop!

I ran to the window and opened the curtain.

WHOOOO-OOOP!

WHOOOO-OOOP!

He was just on the other side of the stone wall, maybe 40 yards away! His voice! The power of the lungs! Amazing and impressive!

Silence.

I stood by the window waiting for more.

A black SUV rolled slowly down the road, turned into my neighbors driveway, and stopped.

Two people that I could see, but couldn't see features. A woman got out of the passenger side and walked to the door of my neighbors home, about 40 yards from my viewpoint at the window. My neighbor was a single woman in her 50's, with a huge 130lb German Shepherd, specifically purchased for her by her boyfriend, for protection. Alphonso. A gorgeous German Shepherd.

With a very deep, intimidating voice.

He started barking. The woman returned to the SUV, got in, and they continued down the road towards the Connoquennessing Creek. I couldn't see if it turned to go up the creek, or continued on to Ellwood City.

That was a head scratcher.

What just happened, and who were those people? Were they somehow connected to the Bigfoot?

I'll just leave it at that and let everyone come to their own conclusions.

Chapter 10 Blobsquatch!

Caption

Why Are There No Clear Bigfoot Photos with Everyone Carrying a Cellphone!

Blogpost
Pennsylvania Bigfoot Project
MARY M FABIAN·WEDNESDAY, JANUARY 10, 2018·

With everyone having a cell phone with camera, just about everywhere, why aren't there any clear photos of Bigfoot? You've got less than 30 seconds, a lonnnng time for a sighting. Get your photo!You're walking or riding in a car. Your mind is elsewhere. In reality, you have 4-10 seconds (or less) to film a figure that is moving away from you. You've got that 4-10 seconds of visibility (or less):
Your heartbeat elevates.
Adrenaline pumps in.
You're shaking because of the adrenaline rush.
Plus you're frightened. This thing is close, 50 yards away, he can get to you and rip you apart in a heartbeat. You're scared out of your wits. You shake more.
Now...
Take your digital camera or cell phone out of your pocket or purse or camera bag. Or your digital DSLR camera with zoom lens is already hanging around your neck on a strap.
Bring it up.
Turn it on.

(Cameraphone) Swipe over to the camera app

Oops! You turned your phone sideways and all the apps suddenly switched places. You brought up the iMessage app! Or.....

Ooops! Your phone went to the lock screen!

Type in your code or press your finger to unlock.

Go to the camera app.

Aim at the figure (if he hasn't already disappeared in the brush).

You try to snap photos.

Auto focus thinks you're taking photos of the branch, bush or leaf on a tree, rather than the figure 30 yards beyond.

Swipe down to video.

Try to focus and zoom where the figure used to be.

You've got a nice clear video of a leaf moving in the breeze, and a blurry blob disappearing into the bush.

Now tell me again why they don't exist because there are no clear photos.

Your cameras auto focus is your worst enemy.

Digital Camera: Put it on Manual Focus.

Even so, Digital Cameras have auto advance, there's a mechanical whine as it advances film, as well as the IR.

Best camera equipment to take if you're out Bigfooting: An old time 35mm film camera. No digital. Put it on a strap around your neck. Have extra batteries and another roll of film.

Think about the best film out there, nice and clear of Bigfoot: The Patterson Gimlin film. Not digital. Not auto focus. Film. No IR.

Try the old 35mm film cameras, as well as an old Super 8 video camera.

The Official Logo & Motto of Pennsylvania Bigfoot Project

"Respect, Help, Share Knowledge, Learn More & Have Fun

PENNSYLVANIA BIGFOOT PROJECT OFFICIAL LOGO

Chapter 12 My Third Bigfoot Sighting

In 2015, my husband and I were looking at properties to build a new home on. We searched in Beaver, Lawrence and Mercer Counties in Pennsylvania, as well as parts of neighboring counties in Ohio.

One day in September 2015, we were driving south on route 7 from Beaver Creek State Park towards East Liverpool Ohio to check out some acreage. My husband was driving, I was the passenger (obviously), looking out the window. We were going about 40 mph. The area was wooded, hills, woods and farmers fields on either side of the road. As we passed a dirt lane on the right, I saw a huge black, husky, broad shouldered Bigfoot walk out of the woods along a trail, cross the dirt lane, and into the woods on the other side. I was in shock. Speechless. About a mile down the road, I asked my husband if he would turn the truck around, that I wanted to look at something. Without question, Lou turned the truck around and drove back until I asked him to pull over, off the road, across from the dirt lane. God Bless Lou! I love that man!

I just sat there and looked at that dirt lane, trying to logically figure out what I had seen.

Was it a deer that I saw? No, way too large and walking bipedal.

Was it a bear? No, much much too large to be a bear, it had long legs, and again, walking bipedal.

Tree Twist & Break Beaver Creek State Park, Ohio

Was it a tree? A stump? No, it moved. Had hair. Arms that swung, and legs that moved in a long stride.

I knew what I saw, and it was a Bigfoot. A huge one.

In January, 2016, I returned to check out that lane. Some construction company had completely torn the area apart.

The woods were gone, a tall 8' razor wire topped chain link fence was up with a gate. No signs, nothing. Just everything gone and changed.

What the site looked like when I returned to investigate 7 months later

Chapter 21 HABITUATION BY GIFTING WITH FOOD

BIG NO NO!

Why It's a VERY BAD Idea To 'Feed' Bigfoot or 'Gifting' aka Habituation By Feeding

Blogpost

Pennsylvania Bigfoot Project

MARY M FABIAN· TUESDAY, OCTOBER 4, 2016

When I first found out that there possibly could be
Bigfoot in my area, I, of course, went to the 'experts'*.
(*tongue in cheek). I hadn't encountered any for 40
years, so I didn't know very much. I received alot of
information and advice. I was advised to place apples,
pineapples, bananas, and peanut butter jars on the game
trail by my property. All the 'experts' agreed, ".... oh yes,
put unopened peanut butter jars by the trail!" Most
everyone said how much success there was in this
practice. Finding open jars, neatly cleaned out. Or the jar
completely missing. I listened, but something about that
advice kept bothering me, so I never did it. More about
this practice at the end of the article.

What is Habituation? In 'Habituating Wild Chimps' from
the Jane Goodall Institute/UK, aka JGI, Mark Wilson
states, "The American Heritage® Stedman's Medical
Dictionary defines "habituate" as "to accustom by
frequent repetition or prolonged exposure." It's a
technical word for a very common psychological
process. When you first hear an unusual sound, say, like
a car alarm down the street, you pay attention to it. But if
the sound continues and nothing much happens,
eventually you ignore it. Habituation is important for
distinguishing changes in the environment and for
differentiating between unimportant or harmless
situations versus potentially dangerous ones. In animal

behaviour studies, habituation specifically refers to the process of getting animals used to people." (1)

Gifting and Feeding your 'Furry Friends' is not Friendly.

It's Dangerous. Do Not Feed the Bigfoot. These creatures are quite capable of feeding themselves, and have been for thousands of years. They don't need your chocolate, your peanut butter, your pizza, your candy. We don't know the affect on their health by giving them human foods.

Primates Share in Human Diseases From Bad Diets

https://www.scientificamerican.com/article/diet-and-primate-evolution-2006-06/

Other primates are close enough to us that they share some of the same diseases that we hairless bipeds aka humans get. Sugar, carbohydrates, may give them diabetes, heart disease, tooth decay. They can't run to their neighborhood dentist to get a tooth filled or pulled. If they get a small toy stuck in their throat, there's no one around willing or able to give them the Heimlich Maneuver. No doctors for heart disease, gum disease, pancreatitis, Crohns Disease, cancer along with diabetes and a multitude of other diseases caused by a bad diet.

What May happen?

And then, if you go on vacation, they're not getting their daily or semi daily 'Fix' of human goodies. They will become violent, there are many accounts of this happening. Ok, they're throwing rocks at your house, or hitting the side of your house. Or worse. Your house gets broken into and trashed. You come home from an evening out to find a back door broken in, huge muddy footprints and brush marks on the walls, wandering all through your home, your children bedrooms. Your family pet left behind for the neighbor to care for, is found literally ripped apart. Your livestock wantonly destroyed. You then discover that you are trapped. You cannot go away. You cannot leave your home because of what may happen. Your neighbors, their families, pets and livestock are now endangered because you wanted to go the easy way to get your photo.

You now have endangered yourself, your family, your pets, your livestock, your neighbors, their families, their pets and their livestock also!

Oh, and what about the Bigfoot?

What happens if you or your neighbor shoots at it because it's getting aggressive when you're late with the feeding. And yes, guaranteed, he will get aggressive. What if you or your neighbor shoots one? Shot, but not killed. Are you with your little 30-06 going to follow the blood trail into the deep woods to put him down? You've condemned him to hours or days of untold suffering. What of his family troupe now? What if the Bigfoot you've been feeding has brought some of that chocolate cake back to his little ones? You've now addicted and endangered an entire troupe.

From JGI, Mark Wilson states, "Most wild animals fear people for good reason: humans are the most dangerous creatures on the planet. But there's little we can learn about the behaviour of wild animals if we only see them running away. In open country, you can sit in your car with your binoculars and watch animals from afar. In savanna parks, where animals have become habituated to cars, you can sit in a Land Rover and watch animals at closer quarters. But in forests, which is where most primates live, there are few roads, and trees block the view from the road anyway. So if you want to study primates, you must go to their "hang-outs." Habituating them to your presence becomes necessary.

The primatologist is much like the cultural anthropologist: he or she seeks to be accepted into a foreign society, not as a member, but as an observer. Primatologists strive to be ignored while they observe and record events. Whether the study subjects are human or nonhuman primates, the new observer may experience a period of intense scrutiny, and may receive both threatening and friendly behaviour before being able to work without altering subject behaviour." (2)

From Mark Wilson at JGI, "Intentionally using food to habituate primates can also pose a risk. Researchers have planted sugar cane to attract wild apes, such as chimpanzees in Mahale, Tanzania, and bonobos in

Wamba, Democratic Republic of Congo. While provisioning makes habituation easier, it does create new problems in that it changes the behaviour of the animals. It is also worthy to note that because primates are our closest relatives, they are particularly susceptible to many of our diseases." (3)

There's a difference between Study and Research vs Trying to Make 'Furry Friends'

Healthy Non-Feeding Habituation takes Time and Patience

From http://www.janegoodall.org.uk/ "In primatology today, scientists seek to study animals without changing their behaviour. This means habituation without provisioning. Not using food means habituation takes longer, and in some cases may be impossible, if for example the study groups are especially wide ranging." (4) "The general rule of thumb is that each individual primate needs about 100 hours to get used to people. In species that travel in cohesive troops, like baboons, every member of the group can see you every time you make contact, so the 100 hours go by fairly quickly, about three months. Chimpanzees take longer to habituate, because the entire social group rarely comes together. Individual chimpanzees often travel alone or in small subgroups, so it can take many years for every member of the group to become habituated. In forest sites, such as Kibale National Park in Uganda or Taï National Park in Côte d'Ivoire, habituation of chimpanzees without provisioning has taken five or six years. " (5)

Remember the saying 'A Fed Bear Is A Dead Bear'? The same applies to Bigfoot. Think about it.

Oh, and about the practice of putting out unopened peanut butter jars? I didn't do it, something just didn't sound quite right about it. Finally, someone with Common Sense jumped into the conversation and gave the right answers that my instincts were correct. Well, Seems that the Bigfoot isn't the

only one capable of opening jars. Raccoons, possums, bear. And if by some chance it is a Bigfoot who opens that jar and cleans it out, what happens to the jar and what remnants of peanut butter inside the jar? Just google photos of animals who have their head stuck in the jars. It's not a funny sight. Think about the torture that animal is going through. Hyperventilating in panic, and not getting enough oxygen. Slow starvation. There is some evidence out there from Bigfoot dna obtained that there maybe a human connection. What if he has a peanut allergy? There is so much harm that can be done to this and other creatures by the practice of 'Gifting' that it isn't worth it.

If you want to study them, do it the way suggested by JGI. With patience. Go out there and just let them get used to you. If they allow it. It all comes down to respect.

And sorry, they really don't need your Friendship. They only need your Respect for them and their Nature. Leave them alone.

RESPECT

If you've started to, and feel this compulsion to continue to feed one, you've set yourself up for a lifetime job. A job that is constant danger. A danger to you. Your Family. Your pets and livestock. Your neighbors. And a Danger to the Bigfoot himself. You are actually hurting them. Not helping them. Respect Them and Their Nature. They don't need you.
They have survived without you for thousands of years. We've gone over this numerous times. If you have any questions, please ask me. There are ways out of this dangerous situation. We can advise.

Reference (1) (2) (3) (4) (5) from Habituating Wild Chimps Habituation is key to observing and researching primates in the wild. Former director of research, Mike Wilson, shares his thoughts based on his work for JGI at Gombe.

http://www.janegoodall.org.uk/chimpanzees/
chimpanzee- central/15-chimpanzees/chimpanzee-
central/25-habituating- wild-chimps

Chapter 14 My Fourth Bigfoot Sighting

Caption

In July 2016, Lou and I sold our home in Beaver County PA, and purchased a 2 acre lot in Lawrence County PA. Almost immediately, I knew there were Bigfoot around. I found various tree structures around our property, and found small footprints in the loose dirt while the foundation was dug.

November 20, 2016, Zhina my Border Collie, passed away. Her ashes are buried on our new property where she loved to lay out of the hot sun.

May 2017, we moved into our new home.

We have a beautiful view from both our front and back porches. One afternoon, I was sitting on my front porch, enjoying the Spring sunshine, looking at the field across the road.

It's a fenced in field, about 8 acres in size, uphill, with woods at the back on the other side of the fence at the back of the field.

At the top of the hill, along the tree line, 3 deer came walking out, walking down between the trees and the fence, then turning into a game trail at the bottom where they disappeared from my view. At the top of the hill, following them, nonchalantly strolled a tall, athletically lean and slim Bigfoot. He was a mixture of mostly grey and brown, more grey on his head with more brown mixed with grey on down to his toes. His long legs swiftly, but not hurriedly, carried him down the hill, along the same path as the deer, where he cut in, onto the game trail behind.

The deer didn't act panicked. They weren't running.

The Big Grey, as I call him, wasn't running either.

I'd estimate his height to be about 7-8' tall. I've since seen him twice more, late at night as he was chasing deer across the back of my property, his grey hair glistening silver in the moonlight.

I've heard vocals late at night, but I don't know if it was him or another male calling a challenge, along with a females inviting vocal.

A neighbor has shown me a photo of other sign in the area also.

I've since seen this same Bigfoot twice more.

One early morning, about 2:30am, I was taking Sinead outside for 'Last Call'. We went out the man door of the garage. I saw a silver flash of something huge running from behind the garage, across the property and into the shadows of the new home on the property next to us. Sinead was in the other part of the yard, and hadn't seen him. Otherwise she would have been terrified.

Another early morning, around the same time as previous, I had put Sinead out, and was standing outside with her. My new neighbors had moved into their home. The husband has a Dodge pickup truck in the driveway. I saw a figure standing next to the truck, head and shoulders above the cab. He had grey hair, shining from the light off of their porch. I realized that either my neighbor was standing on something next to his truck and had suddenly achieved grey hair, or that it wasn't the neighbor. It was the Big Grey standing there.

Chapter 15 Zapped!

INFRASOUND

ZAPPED! Sound Waves, Infrasound, Infrasonic -
Various Reference Articles of Interest

Blogpost for Reference
Pennsylvania Bigfoot Project
Mary M Fabian January 2018

I have gathered together varying articles and scientific studies on Infrasound. Studies on the effects on the body, as well as studies on electronics disruption.
****
****

What is Infrasound? From Wikipedia:
Infrasound, sometimes referred to as low-frequency sound, is sound that is lower in frequency than 20 Hz (hertz) or cycles per second, the "normal" limit of human hearing. Hearing becomes gradually less sensitive as frequency decreases, so for humans to perceive infrasound, the sound pressure must be sufficiently high.
****
****

Volume 25, 2018, Pages 521-533
Chapter 48 - High Frequency/Ultrasonic Communication in Basal Primates: The Mouse and Dwarf Lemurs of Madagascar by Elke Zimmerman

High frequency/ultrasonic communication, defined as communication via vocalizations above 10 kHz, is a rare phenomenon among primates. The nocturnal Malagasy mouse and dwarf lemurs represent an interesting exception. Most, but not all, studied species use the high-frequency/ultrasonic frequency window for communication to cope with various social and ecological challenges in dispersed social networks. By manipulating defined stimuli and behavioral situations, vocalizations can be induced predictably, providing empirical evidence for vocally conveyed emotional states among conspecifics. Findings suggest that in this basal primate group, cross-taxa variation in high frequency/ ultrasonic signaling is linked to predation. Thus, the sensory drive hypothesis postulating that environmental pressures drive the evolution of social signals specifically can be supported. Furthermore, findings indicate that the evolution of high frequency/ultrasonic vocal communication in this primate group represents a compromise between being cryptic for predators and noticeable for conspecifics.

https://www.sciencedirect.com/science/article/pii/B9780128096000000482

****

Sound Waves and Optics
Can sound waves visually distort light waves?
Air Distortions & Refractions - aka 'Portals'
https://en.wikipedia.org/wiki/Acousto-optics - Light refraction & distortion from sound waves They can cause changes in the index of refraction of a medium which can distort light waves. It's called the acousto-optic effect.
Here's a simple video that makes sound visible: What Does Sound Look Like? and this one makes it all fun and games
Any changes in density of air will change light. In aerospace, we studied in lab some sound wave shadows

made by supersonic aircraft. Here are some pretty cool pictures:
http://www.physicscentral.com/explore/action/images/
shockwaves-img2.gif
http://upload.wikimedia.org/wikipedia/commons/7/7b/
Schlierenfoto_Mach_1-2_Pfeilfl%C3%BCgel_-
_NASA.jpg

Sound Waves and Invisibility
Invisibility becomes reality as scientists bend light waves
http://www.scmp.com/news/china/article/1390360/
invisibility-becomes-reality-scientists-bend-light-waves
Engineers make sound loud enough to bend light on a
computer chip   https://phys.org/news/2014-11-loud-
chip.html
****
****

Hollow Transparent Hair - Uses?
Heiligenschein   http://www.atoptics.co.uk/droplets/
heilig.htm
Hollow Transparent Hair - Pennsylvania Skanicum
https://youtu.be/77VzY83HL1w
Polar Bears - Hollow Hair https://www.loc.gov/rr/
scitech/mysteries/polarbear.html
http://it.stlawu.edu/~koon/mar_ref.html
Metamaterials - Silicon based
 https://metamaterials.duke.edu/

Controlling waves in complex media: from time reversal to wave front shaping via metamaterials   https://metamaterials.duke.edu/news/cmip-seminar-controlling-waves-complex-media-time-reversal-wave-front-shaping-metamaterials

Silicon used in metamaterials for cloaking   https://www.memphisdailynews.com/news/2015/feb/28/vanderbilts-valentine-honored-for-cloaking-research/print

Silicon necessary in the diet for bones and hair   "Some people take silicon by mouth for weak bones (osteoporosis), heart disease and stroke (cardiovascular disease), Alzheimer's disease, hair loss, and improving hair and nail quality. It is also used for skin healing and for treating sprains and strains, as well as digestive system disorders."   "A clear function of silicon in humans has not been established. There is some evidence, though, that silicon might have a role in bone and collagen formation."   https://www.webmd.com/vitamins-supplements/ingredientmono-1096-SILICON.aspx?activeIngredientId=1096&activeIngredientName=SILICON
https://www.livestrong.com/article/518021-natural-foods-that-contain-silicon-dioxide/

****
****

How to record it is something that has been expressed.

Here is a Free app for iPhone - I've no idea of the quality.http://downloads.zdnet.com/product/2094-76396366/
Experimental Infrasound Detector http://users.firstva.com/hale/Infrasound.html
The Nature of Sound:· http://physics.info/sound/
Soundwaves http://mysite.du.edu/~jcalvert/waves/soundwav.htm
The Color of Sound http://www.flutopedia.com/sound_color.htm
Schumann Resonance https://www.nasa.gov/mission_pages/sunearth/news/gallery/schumann-resonance.html
Earth's Ohm, 7.83 Hz Deep Theta Binaural Beat (Schumann Resonance for 12 Hours) https://youtu.be/BJ9pkEiI4OQ
****
****

How Do Sound Frequencies Affect the Brain & Physiology
https://cellphonesafety.wordpress.com/2006/10/02/how-do-sound-frequencies-affect-the-brain/
INFRASOUND ITS SOURCES AND ITS EFFECTS ON MAN -- AEROSPACE MEDICAL RESEARCH LABORATORY, WRIGHT-PATTERSON AIR FORCE BASE, OHIO May 1976   http://www.dtic.mil/dtic/tr/fulltext/u2/a032401.pdf
****
****

SINGLE EVENT UPSET - SEU's

SEU - Single event upset   A single event upset (SEU) is a change of state caused by one single ionizing particle (ions, electrons, photons...) striking a sensitive node in a micro-electronic device, such as in a microprocessor, semiconductor memory, or power transistors. https://en.wikipedia.org/wiki/Single_event_upset

Single Event Upset (SEU) Analysis of Complex Circuits Implemented in Actel RTAX-S Field Programmable Gate Array (FPGA) Devices   https://nepp.nasa.gov/files/25566/RADECS2010_Berg_Pres.pdf

****
****

Physics: Waves and Energy http://www.greenwichschools.org/uploaded/riverside/PTA_documents/waves_energy.pdf

Infrasound & EMF   http://walterhutskyjr.com/infrasound-and-emf/

Infrasound and Its Effects on Man -- Wright Patterson AFB May 1976   http://www.dtic.mil/dtic/tr/fulltext/u2/a032401.pdf

http://www.eastcoastrip.org/research-articles/infrasound

Anatomy of an Electromagnetic Wave http://missionscience.nasa.gov/ems/02_anatomy.html

Do Sound Waves Affect Battery Life? https://sg.answers.yahoo.com/question/index?qid=20100402224559AASgeWw

The Inexpensive Infrasound Monitor Project. This infrasound monitor project is designed to make it possible for schools, businesses and amateurs to detect, measure and monitor the infrasound in their environment. http://www.infiltec.com/Infrasound@home/
http://bf-field-journal.blogspot.com/p/theory-bigfoot-cancreate-and-use.html
http://api.ning.com/files/xeV7E6EsoyMges0cfhXFaGWk9zQ89*BDtn0miNlOtz kj70FFehgKYsRrkQlS5jRi9InfpbiGW2MCch8X*aBpU 4qzdnCaJy-D/Fernandez.pdf

Great article on Infrasound, what animals are known to exhibit it, experiments on Lake Champlain and catching an unknown infrasound signature, aka "Champy". As well as physical as well as visual perception effects, that could also explain 'cloaking', etc
http://www.oregonbigfoot.com/blog/bigfoot/nvcode-part-eight-infrasound/

Animal echolocation https://en.wikipedia.org/wiki/Animal_echolocation

Sound Waves, Animals, Communication, and Identification http://www2.gsu.edu/~mstnrhx/Lessons/plan6.htm

Which Birds & Animals Produce Ultrasonic Sound?
http://www.ehow.com/list_6766713_birds-animals-produce-ultrasonic-sound_.html

Symptoms of wind-turbine syndrome might include: headaches SLEEP PROBLEMS night terrors or learning disabilities in children ringing in the ears TINNITUS) mood problems (irritability, anxiety) concentration and memory problems issues with equilibrium, dizziness and nausea   http://science.howstuffworks.com/environmental/green-science/wind-turbines-health.htm

ENT and Allergy Specialists Blog: Can Wind Turbines (Infrasound) Make You Sick? http://www.entandallergyblog.com/2011/03/wind-turbines-infrasound-make-you-sick.html

Can Infrasound (Sound Waves) Make You Sick? http://www.edrabin.com/infrasound.html

Bio-Accoustics We perform research in atmospheric (in the air), underwater, and seismic bio-acoustics. We help major zoos, universities, and students with their own research papers, and conduct our own novel research. http://www.animalvoice.com/bioacousticsr.htm

Infrasound Therapy is still used to this day
http://www.novasonic-therapy.co.uk/works.php

"Mimicking of rhythmic patterns, reproducing vocalizations and the ability to modulate both high and low frequencies consistently are qualities of higher learning capabilities that involve memory. "
Brenda Garrard
https://online.kidsdiscover.com/unit/sound-and-vibration
-reference link
****
****

Effects on Electronics
"As the researchers wrote in the paper, an odd vibration could throw off calculations in at least certain types of quantum computers. The newly designed insulator solves this problem by keeping stray vibrations from traveling through it. At the same time, the conductive, wave-directing properties of its surface might enable new methods of quantum computing, where vibrations along the snowflakes play critical roles in how the computer talks to itself."   https://www.livescience.com/61528-acoustic-insulator-snowflake.html?utm_source=notification
The next cyberattack could come from sound waves
https://theconversation.com/the-next-cyberattack-could-come-from-sound-waves-74716
Do Sound Waves Affect Battery Life? https://sg.answers.yahoo.com/question/index?qid=20100402224559AASgeWw
Waging Doubt on the Integrity of MEMS Accelerometers with Acoustic Injection Attacks   https://

spqr.eecs.umich.edu/papers/trippel-IEEE-oaklawn-walnut-2017.pdf
THE GYROSCOPES IN YOUR PHONE COULD LET APPS EAVESDROP ON CONVERSATIONS   https://www.wired.com/2014/08/gyroscope-listening-hack/
Tractor Beam Levitates Large Orbs with Sound   https://www.livescience.com/61512-tractor-beam-levitates-objects.html?utm_source=notification

INACCESSIBLE WEBLINKS:
There are also studies on how Infrasound / Soundwaves can disrupt the calcium ions in your brain, thus causing the varied medical effects. The thought of which, made me remember ion lithium aka rechargable batteries. Soundwaves do cause ion disruption in the electronics. Thus can cause battery drain.   http://multi-science.atypon.com/.../0263-0923.23.3.159

Chapter 16 My Fifth Bigfoot Sighting

Chuck Schlabs, Myself, Tim "Coonbo" Baker, and Dee Doss at Brown Springs OK

April 2018, my sister, Deborah Parker-McGee, and I were invited to go to Oklahoma with other Bigfoot Researcher friends. Of course, we went!

We were there for a week, an entire week full of adventures, fun, terror, and sightings by almost the entire gang of 14 Researchers.

We got zapped a couple times, were almost surrounded by 3 pissed off Alpha's, I got growled at from something 8' away late one night.

We went to an area nicknamed 'Purgatory' by local Bigfoot Researchers. A scary place, full of history. The guys did some calls, some were challenge calls.

Our Convoy in "Purgatory"

A Bigfoot returned the call from a few miles away to the north and started running in. Another replied to the East, and came running in, calling and roaring all the way. A third replied to the West, and came a'running in on us.

All 3 roaring and pissed, coming in closer, from miles away.

My sister was obliviously safe, playing on her cell phone, in the truck.

The rest of us crammed in closer to one another close by.

The 3 Alpha's came running, came close in, but stopped in the darkness about 50 yards out, hiding behind weeds, brush and trees. They were silent, just observing us, as we guardedly watched them on our thermals.

A half hour went by, silently.

Nothing further happened, they slunk away in the darkness after apparently deeming us to be not a danger or challenge.

It was midnight, and we were 4 hours from the campground, so we figured we'd head back.

We were in a convoy of about 7 pickup trucks. One started having problems with his truck, so they got on the walkie talkie and radioed in that they were going to pull over in the parking lot of a casino. So, we all pulled over. Everyone else got out and gathered around checking under the hood of his truck.

Debbie and I were riding in Dave's truck, with Dave C. and Chuck Schlabs of OK Chasing the Beast, in front, me behind Dave, and Debbie behind Chuck. Dave and Debbie had never seen a Bigfoot, Chuck and I were more experienced. While Dave and Debbie buried their heads in their phones, texting or playing Words With Total Strangers (or whatever that game is called), Chuck and I stayed alert to our surroundings.

Both Chuck and I knew, that no matter where you are, even in the brightly lit parking lot of a casino, you stay watchful and alert. This casino had Bigfoot history. They had been seen by employees emptying trash in the dumpsters behind. Bigfoot handprints and footprints had been taken on and around the dumpster. While the clientele were enjoying the games and buffet inside, the Bigfoot were enjoying the leftovers of the buffet in the dumpster.

And the employees knew about it. And refused to go out back to empty trash after dark.

While Debbie and Dave played on their phones, Chuck and I stayed alert to our surroundings.

Everyone else in our party were gathered around Jim's truck trying to figure out what was wrong.

I was sitting behind Dave, the driver. Chuck was in the front passenger seat, watching out the front window.

Suddenly, I saw a figure running out from between the casino building and the building next door, across the brightly lit parking lot, through the scattered pickup trucks, across the 4 lane highway, onto the median past the speed limit sign, and into the woods.

I was absolutely dumbfounded.

There was a brief moment of silence.

Chuck exclaimed, 'Did you see that?!?' I replied 'Yes! I saw a Bigfoot running....' Chuck and I spoke together, '.... Across the parking lot and into the woods!'

Dave looked up with a blank look, 'What?'

Debbie roused herself from her game, 'What happened?'

We got out of the truck and spoke with the others about it. A security guard from the casino strolled over, so we spoke with her. I asked if a copy of the security camera footage could be obtained? She replied 'No, we'll never give that out. We want our customers to return, and not be afraid to come here, so that footage will be erased. We see them here all the time, but we'll never release any footage.'

Of course, I was deflated by this. Angry and questioning, but I understood why they had to hold that point of view.

After I went home, I was curious about the speed of the Bigfoot. He covered that 76 yards FAST! Both Chuck and I agreed that it was about 3 seconds for him to run that distance.

I later wrote this post in the Pennsylvania Bigfoot Project:

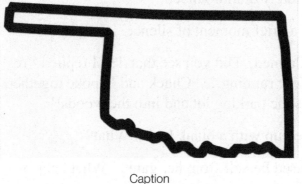
Caption

My April 2018 Oklahoma Bigfoot Casino/Road Crossing
Sighting - Measuring Distance & Time to Estimate His
Speed

It's been bugging me, and I had to figure out the distance
that Bigfoot traveled in 3 seconds, from between the 2
buildings, across the parking lot and road into the trees
on the other side.

Using Free Maps Ruler app, I found out he ran 76.1866
yards, or 228.5598 feet total, in 3 seconds. Which means
that Booger was running about 52 mph.

Our POV was about 90 yards away.

Chapter 17 EMF, Bigfoot, Trail & Game Cameras

You Find an Area that you Suspect is very Active with Bigfoot. You think they pass through this exact spot every night! So, you strategically set up a bunch of Trail/ Game Cameras. You come up with deer, bear, raccoons,

& birds. But no Bigfoot. Or, your camera shows a few photos of interference, blank screens.

It's possible that the Bigfoot, like deer and other game animals, sense the EMF coming off of the cameras. And so, they avoid them. Or disable them using either EMF or Infrasound.
(See my list of many articles on the study and use of Infrasound in the FILES section).

EMF - Electromagnetic Fields (same goes for everyone carrying cell phone cameras) This is a theory that I've been playing around with for a few years, and found an article in support.
Every electronic gizmo puts off EMF. Humans put out EMF.

What Is EMF?
"All electronic devices emit forms of EMFs by passing current through a circuit to perform it's function. Of course, these levels vary based on the purpose of the device but regardless of their function, they are producing some form of EMF and these EMF's are considered 'radiation' which is a byproduct of energy transmission."

This term 'EMF radiation' we hear so much about is most often referring to lower frequency non-ionizing radiation. It's important to understand that there are two types of EMFs.

Chapter 18 There Be Bigfoot

There Be Bigfoot

Blogpost

Pennsylvania Bigfoot Project

Historically, when anyone thinks of the existence of
Bigfoot, they think of the PG film in the Pacific
Northwest. That was my thought, before I knew they
were just about everywhere.

The Pacific NW is considered a 'Temperate Rain Forest',
an area that is prime territory for Bigfoot and other Apex
Predators. The necessities of life abound there. Water,
Shelter, Food.
But, there are more areas of 'Temperate Rain Forest'
throughout the US than we think. From Wikipedia:
"Additionally pockets of temperate rainforest occur in
dreary climates that are not categorized by just annual
precipitation but also number of cloudy days as well as
number of days of measurable precipitation in the form
of rain or snow. In Western North America outside the
Pacific Northwest, the Columbia Mountains of British
Columbia (BC), northern Idaho and northwestern

Montana, have more of a continental climate and have pockets of temperate coniferous rainforest. In Eastern North America, there are scattered pockets of temperate rainforest also exist along the Allegheny Plateau and adjacent parts of the Appalachian Mountains from West

Tree Structure Shenango Twp, Lawrence County PA

Virginia to New England. These areas include sections of West Virginia, Western Pennsylvania, as well as Western Upstate New York and the Adirondack Mountains. A good example of these forests are found in Zoar Valley in Upstate New York (nearest major city is Buffalo, New

Structure, Lawrence County PA

Footprint Lawrence County Investigation

York), Cook Forest State Park within the Allegheny National Forest (nearest major city is Pittsburgh), and Cathedral State Park in West Virginia."

Of course, Bigfoot are found throughout the US, in areas not designated as a 'Temperate Rain Forest'. The struggle for life as an Apex Predator is a bit harder, but they live wherever the 3 necessities of life are. But they thrive in the 'Temperate Rain Forest'.

From AllAboutWildlife: "All apes except for humans live exclusively in or near tropical rain forests. Gorillas, chimpanzees and bonobos (chimp-like, but considered by many scientists to be a separate species) live in the belt of tropical rain forest that girdles central Africa. Some chimps live on tropical grasslands (savannas) adjacent to rainforests." Here in the US, the Bigfoot has learned to adapt in order to survive. They are omniverous, and live close in to cities and feed off of human refuse, along with the occasional careless human, who are easy prey for the deposed and elderly, sick or injured Bigfoot.

Where there are the 3 necessities of life, there are Bigfoot.

Chapter 19 The 10 Commandments of Bigfoot Research

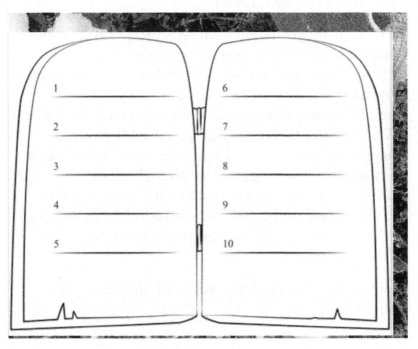

Footprint Neshannock Twp, Lawrence County PA

Blogpost

Pennsylvania Bigfoot Project

**The 10 Commandments of Bigfoot Research
Adapted from & h/t to Palm Beach Research Group**

1. Thou Shalt Be Informed
Before you start an investigation, learn all you can about
the location and the activity that has been reported there.
Seek any books, magazine and newspaper articles that
might have been written about the place. If possible,
interview eyewitnesses to the activity. The more you
know about a location, the better you'll be able to
conduct your investigation. You'll know about specific
areas to look into, the right questions to ask, and will be
better able to understand any evidence uncovered.

2. Thou Shalt Be Prepared
Being informed is part of being prepared, but you should
also be prepared physically and equipment-wise.
Physically, be sure you are feeling well enough to endure
whatever the investigation might demand: climbing,
woods, ticks, dangerous animals, all kinds of weather,

etc. If you have a bad cold, you don't want to spread it among your fellow members or your clients.

Make sure your equipment is ready: plenty of extra batteries, clean camera lens, plenty of memory cards for cameras and camcorders, tape for voice recorders and camcorders, note-taking supplies, flashlights, extension cords.... You should have a checklist of equipment and supplies. Check it and be sure you have everything you need and in good working order.

3. Thou Shalt Not Trespass

Just because you have a well-organized Bigfoot Research group with cool T-shirts does not give you automatic permission to go onto any property or even any cemetery after hours (most are closed after sunset) to do an investigation. Even though a property looks abandoned, the property is still owned by someone, and going into it without permission is illegal.

Always - ALWAYS - get permission to investigate. You can often get special permission to investigate by contacting the owner, if it is privately owned, or from the city, town, or county if it is a public property.

4. Thou Shalt Be Respectful

A big part of your Bigfoot Research group's reputation is based on how respectful it is - to the property being investigated and to any clients that might be involved. A property owner or client is going to want to feel comfortable that your group is not going to be destructive in any way, that the possibility of theft is never an issue, and that you won't be noisy or rude. Treat any client and witness with the utmost respect. Listen to their reports of experiences carefully and seriously. Every member of your group should be especially mindful of this when investigating a private residence.

Be respectful of your team members. Bigfoot Research groups - like all such groups of people - are fraught with infighting, personality conflicts, and differences of opinion. Without respect for one another, your group will fall apart.

Someone else who needs your respect is the investigatee - the Bigfoot. Some investigators take a confrontational approach, being rude and obnoxious when trying to elicit a response from a Bigfoot. Doing knocks & calls without knowing their meaning is disrespectful & idiotic. You're speaking gibberish in a foreign language. They deserve to be treated with the respect you'd give to any large predator.

5. Thou Shalt Not Venture Off On Your Own
We have heard the news reports of investigators who have gone off on their own and gotten seriously injured - even killed. When your team splits up to cover various areas of a location, they should always be in groups of two or more. Safety is a primary reason.

Also, the evidence collected by a person who goes off on his or her own might automatically be suspect. To help ensure the integrity of any evidence, it must be gathered in the presence of two or more people. Which leads us to...

6. Thou Shalt Not Bear False Witness
Or "Thou Shalt Not Fake Evidence." For those who don't know, bearing false witness means lying. And if you're going to falsify, exaggerate, or otherwise alter evidence, then why are you doing Bigfoot Research ? These investigations are about trying to find the truth as best we can.
So falsifying or exaggerating a sighting, manufacturing evidence, Photo-shopping pictures, and other evidence tampering and passing them off as genuine is a Bigfoot Research mortal sin. Why do people do it? For the attention, obviously. But it's counterproductive to the investigation, what the Bigfoot Research group is all about - and just plain wrong.

7. Thou Shalt Be Skeptical
This can often be a difficult thing for Bigfoot Research because we want to find evidence. We want to record a Class A vocal, take a photo, make contact, or otherwise have an experience. That's what drives us to conduct these investigations. But we must take caution and not be too eager. Be honest about that evidence: that vocal could be just the sound of noisy animals or humans in the background.
Be diligent in trying to debunk gathered evidence. Find plausible explanations; do not automatically jump to a

bigfoot explanation. Being skeptical will make any possibly genuine evidence all the more valuable.

8. Thou Shalt Not Covet Thy Neighbor's Evidence
In other words, do not steal from other Bigfoot Research groups. Many groups with websites have found that their evidence - vocals, pictures, etc. - has been "borrowed" by other groups without giving credit where it is due. Do not take evidence from other groups (from their websites or in any other way) without permission. And certainly do not claim it as your own.

9. Thou Shalt Know Thy Limits
It doesn't happen very often, but on occasion a Bigfoot Research investigation can get rather intense. Phenomena might be taking place that you do not have the experience or skills to deal with. Know your limitations on what you are able to handle. You might have to call in or turn over the investigation to a more experienced investigator, particularly if there are physical attacks. Again, these are quite rare cases, but they can happen and you should have a plan for what to do.

10. Thou Shalt Be Professional at All Times
This last Commandment is one that overarches and includes all the others: Be professional. You want your Bigfoot Research group to be respectful and respected, to be honest and forthright, to be ethical and have the highest degree of integrity. Without these things, your

group is doomed to failure and will have contributed little if nothing to the search for truth in this field.

In many endeavors, the term "professional" means that you get paid to do what you do. Of course, that does not apply here. You should be professional in your conduct.

And this leads to a corollary or 11th Commandment: Thou Shalt Not Charge for Thy Investigations.

No group should charge a client for an investigation. Period. Not one dime. In special circumstances, if your group is being asked by a client to travel a long distance to conduct an investigation, the client might offer to pay part of the transportation costs, but this should not be a requirement.

Chapter 20 Various Thoughts

My 5 Personal Rules of Bigfooting:

1. Know your capabilities and limitations.
2. Listen to and Trust your Instincts.
3. Think twice as much.
4. Hear what you are listening to.
5. See what you are looking at.
Re-arranged according to priority.

The Official Motto of Pennsylvania Bigfoot Project

"Respect, Help, Share Knowledge, Learn More & Have Fun"

There is so much more that I've written that I could include here, but you'll just have to join our Facebook Group, Pennsylvania Bigfoot Project to read it.

Caption

We've grown so much over the years, as of the end of 2022, we've got over 17,300 members.

I get asked to speak all over the state and out of state conferences. I set up a vendor booth and sell tee shirts at various Bigfoot and Cryptid related festivals and conferences. If you want one of our logo tee shirts, please contact me at PennsylvaniaBigfootProject@gmail.com for pricing and selection.
I'll send you a link to our shop or if I have your size on hand, I'll mail it to you directly.

Pennsylvania is a huge state, and since I cannot realistically, go everywhere I'm asked to research and investigate all of the sighting reports that I'm given, I've decided to open up County Chapters within the state, along with a few Honorary out of state, and out of country Chapters. Currently, we have over 30 County Chapters up and running that witnesses can report to. We have Campouts that we conduct throughout the Spring, Summer and Fall. No Charge. You just your cost to rent the campsite, your gear, food, etc.

I am proud of what I've accomplished, with God's help and guidance. To Him I give all Glory.

I just pray that other organizations will quit the fighting, the jealousy, the greed, the glory seeking, and start

sharing research discoveries like we, and a few others do.
The more we Share, the more we Learn, the more we will Know.

2 POSSIBLE BIGFOOT
HONOBIA OKLAHOMA
OCTOBER 2022

Caption

In October 2022, my sister, Debbie, and I took another research trip to Oklahoma. This time to the Honobia area, along with Chuck Schlabs, Glen Bourassa and his cousin. We stayed at a cabin owned by a friend of Chuck's. Chuck took us all over the area, where we found structures, etc. But the activity was at the cabin. The morning of our second day there, I went outside, walked around the property and took random photos. I sent them to my Facebook group, Pennsylvania Bigfoot Project where a member told me that I may have something there in one photo. I zoomed in on the photo. And found 2 possible figures.

Chuck and I walked over to the spot where the figures were. We found nothing. No stumps, no trees, no rocks. Just the edge of the bluff where something had laid peeking of the top at me as I walked around.

Throughout our visit, acorns and rocks were tossed at the cabin.

Vocals were heard, unfortunately not caught on audio. Our last night, something walked up to the door and tried the knob. Something else walked up onto the back deck.

Chapter 21

Sinead's Encounter

Salt Fork State Park Campground, Cambridge Ohio
Loop A Site A21
Research Trip
10/12-10/16/2020

Approximately 11:30pm Wednesday October, Amie
Coplan, PBP Team member and head of Monroe County
Ohio Bigfoot, and I returned to camp after a fruitful
evening investigation.
We sat around camp talking about the evening, while
Sinead wandered around us and nearby on her lead.
Her aircraft cable lead is 30' long, shortened to about
20'. It was looped around a tree just over the brow of the
hill, about 7' down the flattened ridge below the fire pit.
Sinead walked to the edge to relieve herself. She was
there for only a moment when she ran back to stand
huddled by me, stretching her lead as far and as tight as

it would go. Her ears were laid back, tail tucked and her eyes looked panicked.

I quickly retrieved the leash, while Amie held onto to Sinead, calming her. I took Sinead to safely & quietly shelter in the truck, comforting and calming her there. She was calmer in a couple hours when we went to the tent for the night.

Nothing could be seen below, and the ground is too packed hard for prints. The hillside is covered in tall, old growth black walnut trees, which heavily and frequently dropped walnuts all around camp throughout our stay. Nothing further happened through the night, except a high wind came through, blowing more walnuts and small tree limbs down.

Sinead tied off on her lead at the Campsite

Chapter 22

Logbook

My Western PA Bigfoot/Sasquatch History From 1960's thru Present

MARY M FABIAN·SATURDAY, OCTOBER 7, 2017

My memory of dates is fuzzy, but my memory of the encounters is clear.

I tried to keep a logbook of activity, but I honestly am really bad at that. I rely on my memory, and anymore, it's not trustworthy. GIGO - Garbage In, Garbage Out.

Summer 1966-1967 What had sparked the initial interest was finding what caused some mysterious experiences I had as a pre-teen in the 1960's., as well as a possible sighting that has haunted me through the years. We lived on a 100 acre farm with horses, sheep, dogs, cats, ducks and 1 rooster in Jefferson Boro, Allegheny County, PA, next to the Thomas Jefferson High School. I'd ride my horse over the trails in back of the farm, just exploring. When I wasn't riding, I'd go out further and hike along a gas line at the far end of the farm. One day, I was walking along this gas line, going further out in the woods. It was a hilly area. This day, I was walking down hill. Directly across from me, about 100' away on the uphill, I saw an extremely tall, extremely large 'man'. I say 'man' because at that time I thought it was a man. although I couldn't discern clothing, it was all black. He was walking across the gas line, out of the woods, into a field on the other side.

He stopped, looked at me, then continued on. This was before the Patterson Gimlin film, and all I had ever heard of were Yeti's and Siberian Snowman. This was probably 1966 or early 67. If it was only a man, I would have forgotten it over all these years, yet it has haunted me ever since. He was so large! Here is a video I made showing an approximation of the terrain and me re-telling what happened. https://youtu.be/vB-VCaEl7r4

Later on, after my dad retired from USS Clairton Works, we'd go camping up in the mountains, and go to a camp in northern PA, at Canadohta Lake. Up in the Laurel Mountains of SW Pennsylvania, I had experienced rocks and acorns thrown at me, hissing when reaching into a berry bush while out hiking, and tree structures, above Uniontown PA while camping and hiking in the backwoods as a teenager with my family 45 years ago. I'd go out hiking alone and walk miles in the backwoods. I'd wake up early in the morning, grab some breakfast, and just take off into the woods and follow the game trails. I wouldn't return until it was almost dark.

By reading and watching various tv programs later on, I found out what caused that, and then sparked a mild, lifelong, but pervasive interest in sasquatch. I even have

3 statues in my front yard, put there, initially, in 2009, long before I discovered what was causing the activity at my home in Beaver County.

I hadn't watched 'Finding Bigfoot' since at that time, we didn't have cable or satellite tv, so I didn't know about the recent 'craze'. So finally, when we did get satellite tv, I watched the show, along with Les Stroud's specials, which got me going onto Facebook pages regarding sasquatch and bigfoot. Some pages are quality, some are just plain bad.

Anyway, as to my more recent experiences:

My husband and I married in late 2004, and I moved into his home in northern Beaver County PA. It's a low slung ranch home, built in the 1950's. My husband installed motion sensor lights on all sides, except for one, the master bedroom end, that he just never got around to putting a motion light in. I would wake up in the middle of the night every so often, startled by a bang on the wall next to my head, or a grumbling, mumbling deep voice. I put it off as the spirit of the former owner, perhaps unhappy that I was there. This continued for years.

June 2014:, I had my grandkids over for the week, and for fun,(stupidly, never realizing the harm) I took them into my backyard, showed them how to do tree knocks and whoops. I've never gone on an 'expedition', and was only going by what I saw on Finding Bigfoot and Les

Stroud Survivorman: Bigfoot series, on how to do this. My grandson did some tree knocks, I taught him to stop and just listen for a reply. NEVER expecting anything. I figured the closest would be Allegheny National Forest if at all. We got a single knock in reply from the woods across the road from my home. No wind. Just a single knock in reply.

2015

February 26, 2015 - Late at night, I'd hear Strange long and drawn out high pitched vocalizations, going from a lower to a higher note. Not coyote.
I heard vocalizations again February 11, 2015, just as I was getting ready for bed. This one was a different type call. The first one for the past few nights was a long, loud shrill howling. The one last night was WHOOO OOOP! WHOOO OOOP! WHOOP About 15 yards behind my home, on Golf Course undeveloped property. Then after that, a long howl from further NNW, the ridge at the other end of the golf course.

Miles of forest, farmland around me, with scattered businesses and homes.
Sorry, no audio. My cell phone was all the way at the other end of the house.

March 2015 I drove up the back road that runs behind

my home, alongside the golf course property. I did a few whoops out the car window.
Later that night: -20F 2:30am I woke up to a violent Banging on the side of the house and something running across the roof. Strangely enough, the only side of the house that doesn't have outdoor motion sensor lights. And the bedroom side of the house. Repeated bangings. No HVAC or plumbing runs on that wall.

May 2015 - Hiking the property behind us. Found a 10" footprint
Sometime between 2007 to 2015 - I had a partial sighting: a hairy head peeking over the stone wall behind my home. Sun was behind him, couldn't make out features. Red gold hair on a very big head.

September 2, 2015 - Wood knock heard from the woods across the road, in response to my vocal 'Whoop'.
September 2015 near Beaver Creek State Park, Columbiana County Ohio. We were driving along, my husband was driving, I was in the passenger seat watching the countryside. We passed a dirt lane in a wooded area. About 100' back, I saw a huge black figure walking across the lane, from left to right, head bent slightly forward, approximately 9' or taller, huge chest. He just about took up the entire lane as he crossed. I wasn't able to get back to that area until 4 months later, and by then, some construction had been done, a wire

fence put up blocking access, so I wasn't able to get in there to do measurements or comparison.

December 2015 - Rhythmic banging on a dumpster located across the road after midnight to 2:00am, 2 weeks in a row, every couple of nights, three bangs every 10 minutes for a half hour or so. Construction crew working at the church during the day.

I notice a 3 week approximate pattern to the banging and my dog very fearfully reacting to something outside.

2016
January 2016 - Security light by my back door was turned so it doesn't trigger.

March 9, 2016 - From Brian Sullivan & our Friends in Montana Bigfoot Project

March 9 2016
WENDIGO ATTACK REPORT
Report details told by: Trapper: Howard B Leblank, a 54 year old trapper and hunting guide from Kenora Ontario. This tale was told to Howard when he was a boy by his father a French Canadian fur trapper, from when he worked the area north east of Huntsville Ontario as a boy before Algonquin Park was a managed area. At that time

the lumber trade was very active in the area. Leading to an influx of hunters and fishermen whom used the logging roads to gain greater access to the deep wilderness areas.

A father and son from Chicago Illinois, by the family name of Sears on a hunting trip for moose in the greater Mattawa river region. Guided by an Algonquin Indian / French Canadian Guide, Little Jack. (probably a nick name).

The guide little Jack was a Guide of some reputation in the region whom was known for putting hunters onto large moose and was much sought after, having made a name for himself guiding Rich tourist and visiting politicians from across Canada and the United States.

The year was 1894, the exact location was a lake (name withheld). Season October, Rutting season for moose. The best time to hunt bull moose, which congregate at that time of year to battle for dominance in the mating season.

The hunters and guide paddled the main trunk of the Mattawa River along the Ontario – Quebec border taking a branch creek north into Quebec. On this two day trip many moose were seen but the Sears where looking for a true trophy and pressed Little Jack to take them deeper into the wild region. With hesitation Little Jack agreed to take them to a lake he knew of but explained to them that they would stay only in that area during daylight hours and would be departing by mid day as he had fears of some large beast that was reputed to frequent the area. The Sears took as superstition and largely discounted Little Jacks warnings.

On arriving at the lake Little Jack, laid down the ground rules for the days hunt. He instructed the Sears to stay on the south side of the lake and placed the father in a thicket overlooking a clearing that was bordered by the lake. The son was to canoe along the lake to the east and set up his hunting blind along a marsh area. Both men promised they would not cross the lake which was not wide at that point and the guide would go between the two men frequently. Little Jack was nervous and spent a great deal of time that morning being sure his charges were staying in they're assigned hunting spots. At about noon Little Jack told Mr. Sears senior to begin to get ready to leave promising to bring them back early the next morning. Then began to turn to leave but Mr. Sears Senior then pointed out to the lake. Little Jack turned to see young Mr. Sears paddling across the lake already very close to the other side. Little Jack began to run yelling and waving trying to get young Mr. Sears to turn around but the young man either did not hear him or chose to ignore him. It was at this time Mr. Sears Senior notices a large shape moving in the tree line along the shore of the opposite side of the lake. Thinking it was a moose he called out to little Jack whom at this point was about to land his canoe. Little Jack was frantic and turned to tell Mr. Sears Senior to remain silent. Getting into the Canoe little Jack began to paddle as quickly as possible. But by this time Young Mr. Sears was already landing and pulling his canoe up onto the opposing shore line. Little Jack again tried to call young Mr. Sears back but the young man ignored his calls and walked into the woods. In the time it took for little Jack to cross the lake he heard the reports of young Mr. Sears rifle as several shots were fired followed by silence for a moment. As Little Jack was about to land his Canoe. Young Mr. Sears came running out of the tree line as if being pursued. Little Jack had no time to land his Canoe but raised his own rifle firing to shoot what ever might be chasing young Mr. Sears. A large upright hair covered beast emerged from the tree line after young Mr. Sears. In a few short steps the beast was upon young Mr. Sears and the beast reportedly decapitated the young man by grabbing him by the upper torso from behind and then with it's other hand simply twisted the young mans head off.

Little Jack emptied his gun at the beast, but the beast did not fall instead it carried the body of Young Mr. Sears back into the woods dragging the body by a leg and carrying the young mans head in his other hand.

Little jack having no more ammunition returned to Mr. Sears Senior.

It is reported that Mr. Sears Senior insisted on going after the beast having witnessed the entire event from his vantage point on the opposing side of the lake. But Little Jack refused and almost had to drag the distraught Father away from the area.

When having reached they're camp at the Mattawa river Little Jack insisted they pack and paddle to the nearest settlement which they reached by the following morning.

It was reported to a local constable whom led a search party that included both little Jack and Mr. Sears Senior and several loggers and woodsmen to the lake where they searched for several days finding only Young Mr. Sears broken rifle and a short trail of blood at the actual area of death of young Mr. Sears. It is reported that the searchers all heard beastly screams and howls on those nights when the search would be suspended do to the coming of darkness and eventually they all gave up in fear as each night the screams and howls seemed to be closer to their camp.

Aftermath: Little Jack moved to the Huntsville area after that trip his reputation ruined, he made his living trapping and fishing and was said to have become an alcoholic, drinking away his money when he had any and living off land but never to far from town.

Story report taken by Suzy.

February 26, 2016 - I am pretty well convinced that the government knows and is actively tracking and studying the bigfoot. I've heard Brenda Harris talking about this, and I witnessed similar happenings also, where a mysterious black vehicle came racing in, pounding on my neighbors door, not 10 minutes after that booger whooped and went through our yards to get to the rutting female bigfoot. I guess he got away from their area and they had to really hustle to track him. This was one year ago, this month.

March 2016 - Security light by my back door turned so it doesn't trigger.

April 19, 2016 - We discovered that our midnight visitor is still coming around. He's adjusting the security light on the eaves, so it won't come on in the backyard.

We have security lights on our home, to deter anyone or anything from coming too close to the house. As I told in a previous post (seen in the Files section), we were missing one light on the bedroom end. My husband put one at that end of the house the day after the harassment from the bigfoot overnight, beating on the siding and jumping up on the roof. He still occasionally comes around, since my husband works on the road at times. He'll move the security lights before full dark, if I'm not watching, so the lights won't turn on when something comes to the edge of the yard.

May 2016 - Security light by my back door turned so it doesn't trigger.

We moved in July 2016, about 10 miles north as the crow flies, on 2 acres, adjoining woods and farmland. We are further out in the country, farmland, woods for hundreds of square miles. September 2016, looking around the foundation of our new home as it was being built, I found a trackway of 2 individuals, smaller, perhaps juveniles. The stride was 21' long, so they must've been running, perhaps chasing deer, or just running to get out of the open.

June 27, 2016 - The crows have been chattering like all heck. Then I just heard a knock. Across the road from my home. Left upper is the street light. Mid right of the photo, there's a deer trail entering the woods, crossing over from my land across the road to the woods across.

I was working in the yard, when I heard the crows going nuts over there. Then I heard the knock. A little while later, I could hear the crows moving, still making noise, crossing the road, to the wooded area above my home and on up the hill.

December 4, 2016 - Moraine State Park, Butler County PA Investigation

Louis Fabian and I did a pre-investigation of an area in Western PA where several reports of sightings and encounters have happened. On this day, it's hunting season, so we stayed on the outskirts, but it's an area that we will return to when hunting season is over. Tree structures found, twists and bends.

2017

Spring 2017 At my new home, observed a tall lanky figure walking inside the treeline, about 50 yards behind a small herd of deer. The figure was about 300' away, inside the treeline, could not make out details, impression of greyish brown hair. Taller than my neighbor who is about 6' tall. **Spring 2017** Heard a vocal just before coyotes started up. Heard a single YIP, then silence. Possible Bigfoot coyote hunt & kill.

March 21-26, 2017 - March 21 thru March 26 The Bigfoot Outlaws Meet & Greet at Land Between the Lakes, Kentucky, Redd Hollow Campground

Day 1 - Tuesday, March 21
My sister, Deborah Kay Parker-Mcgee and I drove down from Western PA. I left my home at 3:00am EST, picked her up at 5:00 EST, and arrived at 3:30pm CST at our cabin outside of Dover TN, at the base of the Trace road running north/south through LBL. After settling in, I ran up to the campground, about a 35 minute drive, and introduced myself to Coonbo, Clint, Mark Newbill, Shelley Hutchens Read, Larry Porch II, Vicki Fulcher & Dan Ricke, and so many others already there. We drove back to the cabin, ate dinner, watched tv, then went to bed. I woke up at 4am to a banging on the wall by the window. Plumbing? Could be. I hope so.
Day 2 - Wednesday, March 22 - A LONG DAY
Debbie and I got up the the campground about noon, and met the rest of the crew. I finally got my Bear hug, which

made my day! We sat around the campfire and gabbed, got to know one another. Coonbo asked if we wanted to come along to see the sites of the bowhunter and RV attack. Of course, we said Yes! So, Deb and I climbed into Coonbo's 4WD. We went to the site where the bowhunter was killed. Then we went to the old abandoned campground used to be, where the family was killed beside their RV. I cannot begin to tell you of what the feeling is in either of those areas. Evil still permeates the land. You feel sick to your stomach from the fear, the abject terror and pain that was suffered there. I'll post a link to the telling of the attack on the family at the campground in the comments below. There were scraps of old bottles, wire, the remnants of electric hookup. Someone picked up a scrap and was going to take it home as a souvenir. I suggested that with all of the evil done there, something may be carried home along with it. He dropped it. Kain and Coonbo found a Bigfoot trackway running next to the site out of the gully.

We went to a historic site of an old country RC church. We ran back to the campground, picked up a few more people and then drove back out for an outing to a couple of really deserted areas. Clint, Coonbo's son, consulted the map, while Coonbo drove us down the highway, to a gravel road where we turned, then again onto a rutted road, where we bumped and jostled our way. We continued down to what looked like a wide deeply rutted path, where we followed it down into a deep holler, where we stopped by a field. Coonbo gave out a call, and we stopped and listened. No response. Someone else gave out a call. No response, only the spring peepers. A few more calls, with no response, the flashing of flashlights out into the fields, then all piled back into the trucks, and continued on to another site that was deeper down than the previous. We rocked and slowly rolled down a very very deeply rutted track, turned the vehicles so that we were pointed back out for a possible speedy egress. Again, a few calls, flashlights looking into the woods for eyeshine. Nothing was out that night, in those areas. We drove back to the campground.

Debbie and I got into my Outback, and drove back to the cabin, and tiredly fell into bed at 5:00 am.

Day 3 - Thursday, March 23

...... And woke up at 8:00am to a pounding on the solid wood door of the cabin. Debbie's room was closest to the door, so she crawled out of bed and asked "Who is it?" A man replied in a deep voice "It's the County Sheriff. I'm here to ask a couple questions."

Debbie asked him to walk over the window on the porch, to show his uniform and badge. He did, so she opened the door. By that time, I had rolled out of bed and had walked over to the door in my flowered pj bottoms and tee shirt. The officer was a youngish man, black hair and glasses. He peered in at me. "Who all is in there?" He asked. Debbie replied "Just my sister and myself." He asked, "Did you happen to hear or see anything unusual yesterday?" I thought about what we did the previous day, and just about burst out with a giggle, but re-thought that response. I told him, "No, we were away all day, and didn't get in until 4 or 5:00am this morning." He blinked and repeated, "4 this morning?" I nodded an affirmative. He apologized for disturbing us, and thanked us, then walked off the porch. We closed the door, and just looked at one another in puzzlement. Then said, heck, we'll check with the lodge owner later. Then we went back to bed.

By that time, I was awake, though, so I couldn't sleep. I got back up, made myself some coffee and oatmeal, and watched tv until Deb got up.

After Debbie got up, and we were showered and ready, we drove out, but stopped at the lodge and asked what happened. Apparently, another guest, a young man, had rented a cabin. He went out for a job interview, and returned to his cabin. He called the cops and reported it had been ransacked, torn apart and money missing from under the mattress where he said he had hid it. The lodge owner went up and spoke with the young man. The cabin did not look in the least to be 'tore up' nor 'ransacked'. And the story changed. Money was missing from a drawer. Everyone agreed that the young man was attempting to con everyone into letting him stay in the cabin for free. He was told to leave.

Deb and I headed back up to the campground.

Bear informed me that I was riding along with him that night. Debbie declined, so that evening, before it got dark, she took the car back to the cabin, and spent a relaxing night there. I rode along with Bear and about 7 others in 2 vehicles, including Mark Newbill, Dan & Vicki, Sherrill Corntassel, Paul Husley, Dave Counts, Bear and myself. Bear's strategy was to drive to one area, set up a campfire, cook some bacon, and just act natural. So we did. Mark set up his audio recorder, I had left mine in the car, so I used the voice recorder app on my phone. Paul had what he called 'Game headphones', that he loaned to me to wear. They're used to muffle gunshots while target practicing, but amplify voices and other sounds. I put them on, and immediately could hear bipedal footsteps in the woods. The headphones amplify sounds either immediately in front and behind you. I couldn't tell which direction the footsteps were coming from. About an hour in, a Whoop came from the woods behind us. We acted as if we didn't hear it, and continued to laugh and joke and cook bacon in the fire. A couple hours later, I thought I heard another whoop from further away. I'm hoping that it was picked up by Mark's recorder. My review of my own recording yielded only us talking, no whoops. Bear got a text message from his wife that a windstorm was blowing in, and wreaking havoc on the camp, so we packed it up early, at 1:30, and drove out. Bear drove me down to the cabin and I waved good night, very very tiredly.

Day 4 - Friday, March 24 The Meet & Greet Officially Starts

I slept well, but woke up at 8:30am. Debbie and I drove up to the campground about 2:00pm. Since it was Friday, during Lent, I had brought a batch of Seafood Chowder that I had pre-made. We set up the table top grill on the ground, next to the concrete picnic table, so that it was sheltered from the wind gusts, and fired it up. We put the chowder on to heat up and sat & gabbed with Vicki.

When the soup was warmed up, we got the dixie bowls & plastic spoons out and let any and all know to come 'n get it! New arrivals wandered in and were greeted warmly with hugs and a bowl of seafood chowder. The kettle was empty in a couple hours, with many having 2 and 3 bowl fulls, so I guess it was a hit.

That evening, everyone set up a circle around a campfire in a more sheltered area, with a nice crowd of about 40 or 50 people. Coonbo and Bear introduced themselves, along with the other Outlaws who were present, then fielded some questions.
Peck made one of his infamous 'siren' calls. That man has some serious lung power!
It was a wonderful evening, bundled up in the chill air, but wonderful!
Day 5 - Saturday, March 25
A drizzly morning, but it cleared up. It was pretty much same as the day before. We wandered down to the campfire meeting area and gabbed. Little by little, people wandered in, and set up their chairs. It drizzled a little bit, but only for a little while, and not enough to chase anyone away.
Valerie Guice found the coyote that met an untimely end, and took a photo. It was twisted like an old dishrag. You'll need to ask her about it.
Kain & Eric went for a hike, found the coyote along with a few tree structures. They deliberately peed on the structures to elicit a response.

Which we got later.

It was an evening spent talking about encounters and adventures. Some strange noises or vocals were heard, and since I was facing the creek and woods, I spotted eyeshine pretty far back, I couldn't tell from what side of the creek. Vicki took her 'Bionic Ear' and sat away from the crowd, to see if she could hear anything else.

Nothing further happened that evening. Except for Coonbo's encounter by his generator. That story is his to tell, and it's on a few podcasts. No one wanted it to end. It was an evening of tears, hugs and good byes and sharing of emails and phone numbers.

Deb and I left about 10:30 for the cabin. Bittersweet. We didn't want it to end.

Day 6 - Sunday, March 26

We were packing up the car, when a loud 'HOOT!' came from the deeply wooded holler behind the cabin. Debbie ran into the cabin. I stepped inside and shut the door. Another 'HOOT!' I told Deb that it was an owl.

So, we finished packing, and left the cabin about 5:30am. We stopped for a breakfast sandwich at the McDonalds drive thru, gassed up, and headed home in the drizzling rain.

Heavy downpours all throughout Kentucky, slowed us down to a crawl. We stopped for lunch at the Cracker Barrel, then continued on. We hydroplaned next to an 18 wheeler who was creeping over into my lane, just outside of Wheeling WV. That was an 'Oh CRAP!' moment.

At 4:00pm, we met Debbie's husband, Curt, just off of I-79 at Racetrack Road, by the Meadows, at the Wendy's, where they unpacked her stuff from the jumbled mess in the back of the car, and I continued on. I got back to the apartment about 7:30pm.

Coonbo had an encounter while packing up his trailer, and that is his to tell, on a few podcasts talking about this trip to LBL.

From what I hear, since this Meet & Greet went so well, everyone behaved themselves (after dire warnings), the Outlaws are currently planning next years 'Meet & Greet'.

I hope they continue, because I plan on attending. Most definitely!

Thank You, Bigfoot Outlaws!!! Thank you for sharing not only your stories, encounters and adventures. But I want to Thank You for sharing your Wisdom and Knowledge of these creatures, and willingness to teach others to Respect them.

Anyone wanting to learn more, please do so with an open mind and respect. Just do a search for the group Bigfoot Outlaws Hideout. Or join my group, Pennsylvania Bigfoot Project.

Until Next Year!

May 2017 - Checking out the area in the back of our property where sticks were thrown at me last year, and running light bipedal footsteps away from me, to my right, to a more densely wooded area. There's a gully with a Creek just behind the dead tree, with an upslope on the other side leading to the farm behind me.

There are tree limbs stuck up in a possible formation. I checked, the broken limb did not come from the trees that it's wedged in, and there is no broken stump below or to the side. The long end is jutting into my property, into bushes, facing the field and my home about 50 yards away. Sentry point? My puppy was Very interested in the smells beneath. And how could I forget, I found 3 footprints from 2 individuals by my foundation last year also. — at Shenango Township, Lawrence County PA

June 1, 2017 Approximately 10:30 pm, I was sitting on the porch with Sinead, my BC puppy. She's about 3 months old. From over the hill, we could hear a large dog barking. Then for a few seconds, quiet. Sinead got up, walked forward so her head was sticking out between the porch spindles. She stared intently at the wood line on top of the hill across the road from us. She started softly growling. She started backing up towards me, still softly growling, until she was up against my legs. My weak little 100 lumen flashlight did basically nothing. I gathered my things, grabbed her leash, and we retreated into the house.
I praised Sinead & petted her. This is one reason why I got her.
She's my early warning system.

June 12, 2017 The man we hired to brush hog the field behind the house reported a tree limb thrown at him, hit and landed on his mower deck, he was about 15' from the treeline.

July 2017 I explore the woods beside and behind my home. Tree structures, bows, and other things noticed consistent with BF activity.

July 21, 2017 - Sinead and I went on a preliminary hike today to Hells Hollow at McConnell's Mills, Lawrence County PA where we've received reports. We'll go back once the weather cools & less greenery around.

No sighting, but possible sign of tree structures found. And bonus, we were able to cool off at the waterfall. I only walked as far as the falls, .04 mi. That's about all my hip could take, there & back. My hip/leg injury is from stepping into a groundhog hole about 13 years ago

August 2017 Bionic Bird call heard 8:30 am from inside the treeline across the road from my home. Long, drawn out slightly wavering high note whistle/call, lasting about 7-10 seconds, then short drop to a lower note.

I heard it this morning, as soon as I took my pup outside. I heard something else immediately after. Any ideas of what it could be, other than what I suspect? And honestly, I'd be relieved if it's not what I suspect. I heard a similar call from Dan Ricke at LBL in March on one of our night outings.

2018

January 2018 Another Bionic Bird call, different location, woodline behind my home.

April 2018 We (my sister, Deborah Kaye Parker-McGee & myself) travelled to Oklahoma where I had another sighting, where a Bigfoot ran across a brightly lit parking lot. We were invited on a research trip in Oklahoma by Coonbo Baker. So, we packed up and took the long drive out. While there, our group had many vocals, saw tree structures, footprints, and other members had sightings also. Chuck Schlabs and Tim "Coonbo" Baker talk about our sighting on Chuck's podcast, OK. Chasing the BEAST.

I appear on Chuck's podcast later on, and we talk about it there also. On Thursday, I think it was April 7 - will need to double check on that date, our group of 14 researchers went to an area euphemistically nicknamed 'Purgatory'. We were there during the daytime, saw sign and decided to return later that night. We went to dinner, then our caravan of 7 vehicles returned to Purgatory. We saw eye shine, heard vocals from Bigfoot coming in on us from different directions, heard something up in the bushes up on the hill above us. After a fun evening there, after the activity died down, we drove out. One of our group was having some engine issues with his pickup, so we all pulled over into the parking lot of a casino. We had stopped at this particular casino earlier, because Bigfoot were regularly spotted behind the casino by the dumpsters, reported by staff, who refused to take the trash out at night time out of fear. Everyone else in our caravan were helping the gentleman on his truck, but the 4 of us in Dave's pickup were too tired. We were parked facing the casino from the side, with the dumpsters on our left. Dave was the driver, Chuck in the front passenger seat, myself behind Dave on the drivers side, and my sister, Debbie, behind Chuck in the rear passenger seat. Dave and Debbie were both looking at their cell phones. Chuck and I were idly looking out the windows. *Neither Dave nor Debbie at that point in time, had ever seen a Bigfoot. We were always ragging them to get off their phones. Suddenly, on the left, from between the casino and the next building, out comes a Bigfoot, running bipedal, full tilt, arms pumping, running across the parking lot, between the pickup trucks and under the bright lights. His head was above the pickup trucks. He ran across the parking lot, across the 4 lane highway, past a speed limit sign, and into the woods. Silence for an instant .....

Then Chuck exclaimed "Did you see that!" I replied "Yes I did! A Bigfoot ran across ..." and together we said where it came out, where it ran and where it ran into the woods. We together agreed that it took him about 3 seconds to run that distance. We estimated by the speed limit sign that it was about 8' tall. Later on, I got on Google Maps, found a piece of software that I could precisely measure from Point A to Point B. I took the time of 3 seconds, vs the distance and estimated the speed that he was running at approximately 52mph. When I find the post where I give the exact distance, I'll add that on here.

April 17, 2018 Facebook Post

Not all groups are out to 'Prove' the existence to doubters, unbelievers and skeptics. We leave that up to other groups,and to the doubters themselves to work thru. Our tactics in gathering evidence may not be to everyones satisfaction. Our aim is research and studying the Bigfoot biology, anatomy, habitat and behavior. We are into the science of Bigfoot. Our aim is to learn more, and to share what we learn. That's the official answer. Truthfully, Heck, we just plain have fun in what we do. We enjoy it. We enjoy being out in the woods. The camaraderie, adventure and discovery. The search and the glimpses and full sightings. The shock and discovery of someone who has never seen one, finally having their first encounter and sighting. That is what we enjoy. We have FUN. We have fun while we're learning. And maybe that's a big part of it. Just the joy, fun and adventure of the search.
We know of their existence, of that there is no doubt. We've seen them multiple times. I've seen 5 and have had encounters too numerous to count. The people we research with have experience and researched over 40

years with multiple sightings. Including Scientists, as well as other specialties.

We are based in Pennsylvania, but we research out of state also. Our focus is on the science of the entire creature. Casting of footprints is important, yes. There's alot to learn about them from the study of the footprint. When you are way out in the bush, sometimes it just isn't feasible to carry extraneous equipment and heavy casts. Especially when you are traversing muddy, log and limb strewn areas with rattlesnakes, copperhead and cotton mouth in the area.

I appreciate your understanding of this and no hard feelings. Our respect goes out to all other researchers who work hard in this endeavor.

Thank you.

November 2018 Pennsylvania Bigfoot Project & Seeking Ontario's Bigfoot were called in to investigate possible Bigfoot activity on private property near the Allegheny National Forest PA.

2019

January 8, 2019 - The other night while I was outside with Sinead, my Border Collie, she zeroed in on something in the side yard and started barking like crazy. She's almost 2 years old, and small, maybe 30 lbs soaking wet.

We have a fenced in area for her off the side of the garage. She's never alone out there at night. I turned the light over there and saw eyeshine low to the ground creeping forward towards our fence. About 50' away. I couldn't see it clearly, just something low belly crawling up on us. It didn't look overly large, anywhere from 4' to 6' long. I called her back inside. When we went back out later it was gone.

Could have been a coyote, which are numerous in the area.

2020

July 19-26, 2020 - Pennsylvania Bigfoot Project 3rd Annual Group Campout

DAILY LOG

Pennsylvania Bigfoot Project 3rd Annual Campout

Quemahoning Family Recreation Area In Holsopple PA.

SUNDAY

Sunday, Deb & I arrived & set up our camp on site # T14 by the lake. The first photo is our view from our table by the fire pit.

George Workman arrived Sunday and set up his hammock on T11 also with a nice view of the lake. He'll relate what he did and found.

Sunday Evening: Sitting by our campfire, I heard a possible whoop, but it was all the way on the opposite side of the lake. Too far & quick to be sure.

MONDAY

Monday, during the day, Deb & I went scouting to the north for potential areas to hit up at night, George did so also in the other direction. On our previous trip here, I found a couple areas with great promise close to the lake. Monday night after dinner, George, Deb & I, along with Larry Gamble, decided on one area next to the lake.

Deb, Larry and I went in my truck, while George travelled in his car to the area. We pulled in, turned our vehicles so they were pointed out and set up our chairs. George placed an audio recorder inside the woodline. We settled in to wait as it got dark.

At full darkness, we moved around, spoke and acted as if we were just there to star watch. Very casual and relaxed. We watched as a mentor shot overhead, and the stars came out beautifully in a clear sky. The temperature was comfortable in the mid 60's.

We listed as two bullfrogs sang at opposite ends of the inlet, across the road from us.

Slowly, we heard surreptitious tree snaps as something moved in the tree line behind us. An occasional snap beside us, 30 yards away. The bullfrogs went silent as a third moved between them on that side of us.

An occasional tweet of a bird further back in the woods. An owl hooting.

The movement continued to hold our attention.

The thermal imager couldn't see beyond the tree line with the thick brush.
All we could do was listen.
Little by little the noises stopped.
They tired of playing, and we were tired. George retrieved his recorder and we returned to camp for the night.
TUESDAY
Heavy rains in the afternoon, scattered into the evening. We postponed the evening follow up investigation.
Heavy showers forecasted for today, from 11-5. We'll see how it goes.
WEDNESDAY
Rain this morning, will update after we go out this evening on follow up investigation.
Evening: 5 of us went out to follow up in the same area as the previous nights investigation. Very little interaction, but both Larry & Stacey spotted possible eyeshine in the areas they were watching. Movement was heard in multiple areas. Stacey reported hearing a low pitch steady hum that she could feel in her chest. Possible infrasound "zap".
Steve Surmick & Stacy Surmick, Larry Gamble, Deborah Kay Parker-Mcgee & myself.
THURSDAY
8:00 pm: Moriah Ross & her daughter, Stacey, Patrice, Lauren, Lupe & her son, & Larry, came along with Deb & I to the same turnaround area that we've had activity at for the past few nights.

Moriah & her daughter went into the woods looking for sign. They found prints, tree bends & had other exciting activity that Moriah will share photos.

We heard movement all around us again, but could not see anything on the thermal or night vision because of the thick cover. The movement was intermittent & surreptitious. Drawing our attention one way while they moved to another spot to watch us. The activity was less than what we had experienced previously.

Near the end of the evening around 11:00, a rock came flying thru the upper trees to land on the hiking trail entrance, about 60' away from where we were set up. Moriah and her daughter were still out but I could see their location by their flashlights. A salamander was thrown at Moriah's daughter. It was missing its tail & had a head injury. Photo below.

The normal night sounds returned, so we knew they were done.

FRIDAY

Night- The guys from Catskills Bigfoot were out exploring & filming their podcast. Patrice, Deb & I went to the bridge area to see if it was as good as it looked. Perfect area to call blast, but there were fishermen all around, so we didn't stop. We went back to the turnaround area & waited for the CABC guys. Nothing happened there, I think the youngsters got bored with playing with us. Eventually we went back to camp. The night was a bust.

SATURDAY

Our day to get together in camp with everyone who was left in camp, as well as those who could drive in & talk Bigfoot. Most everyone had packed up & left Friday. Colleen Margaret Tippie & Her husband, Dennis drove down, and we had a very nice visit. We all went to dinner at 5:00 at the Flyin' Lion Restaurant in Jennerstown. Got back to camp to say goodbye. Thank you Colleen & Dennis! You made our day!

SUNDAY July 26
It's 7:51 am- I'm enjoying the peace & quiet of the morning. Time to pack up & go home.
I hope more of you can join us next year!

Thank you, to all of you who were able to make it to this years Group Campout! I enjoyed meeting new friends, seeing old friends & enjoying great companionship in this endeavor!
To Next Year!

October 2-4, 2020 Coshocton County, Ohio

On a Bigfoot Campout with my Ohio friends, hosted by SOSBI and Doug Waller.
I arrived in camp Friday late afternoon and set up my tent inside the tree line apart from most everyone else. Three others put their tents up there also, but we were about 30 yards apart from one another. I was able to back my pickup to within 10-15 yards of my tent.

Friday Night: We went down to the dam and another area where previous sightings happened. Nothing, no sounds, no calls. FREEZING! In the 30's, so I slept in my truck cab. Woke up about 3:00 am to a shriek/scream close to my truck. I unfortunately had not put my audio recorder out. And none of the others had caught that particular audio.

Saturday: Walking around my tent, I found footprints. There was a log behind my tent where something had stepped and scraped the moss off. A few feet beyond, were a couple footprints. Not deep enough to cast. I called a few of the others over. Photos in the album.

Saturday Night: SOSBI meeting with about 30 people in attendance, gathered around the campfire. Doug Waller went over sighting reports and we talked about what we had found at the camp so far.
After the meeting, a few of us went back to the dam with a few new people who had attended the meeting. We showed them how our thermal and night vision worked. Nothing there again. The group split up, with some hiking at another location, and our group going to another location where a sighting had happened. Three of us had our thermal vision / FLIR's and looked around. One person saw something across a pond. It didn't show on my therm, or the others. He watched it for awhile, but it didn't move. When he looked again, it was gone. Possible heat signature left over from the daytime on a tree or rock that faded as the night cooled. Something very large rushed thru the brush away from us into the trees when a couple of us turned back to our trucks. At that point, everyone turned to look where the sound came from, I turned and looked in the opposite direction in case it was a diversion. I didn't want anything coming in on us and hiding

under one of our trucks. No other sounds for the night. Video taken at that location.

Sunday morning: We broke camp, packed up. One member reported his trailer getting rocked during the night, along with hearing something walking in, moving his chair on the concrete pad. We could find no handprints on the side of his trailer.

2 3/4 hour drive home.

October 12-16, 2020 - Salt Fork State Park

Co-Investigation with Amie Coplan of MW/PBP Team, PBP and Monroe County Ohio Bigfoot went to Salt Fork State Park Ohio from 10/12-10/16/2020.

Approximately 11:30pm Wednesday October, Amie Coplan, PBP Team member and head of Monroe County Ohio Bigfoot, and I returned to camp after a fruitful evening investigation. We sat around camp talking about the evening, while Sinead wandered around us and nearby on her lead.
Her aircraft cable lead is 30' long, shortened to about 20'. It was looped around a tree just over the brow of the hill, about 7' down the flattened ridge below the fire pit.
Sinead walked to the edge to relieve herself. She was there for only a moment when she ran back to stand huddled by me, stretching her lead as far and as tight as it would go. Her ears were laid back, tail tucked and her eyes looked panicked.
I quickly retrieved the leash, while Amie held onto to Sinead, calming her. I took Sinead to safely & quietly shelter in the truck, comforting and calming her there. She was calmer in a couple hours when we went to the tent for the night.

Nothing could be seen below, and the ground is too packed hard for prints. The hillside is covered in tall, old growth black walnut trees, which heavily and frequently dropped walnuts all around camp throughout our stay.

Nothing further happened through the night, except a high wind came through, blowing more walnuts and small tree limbs down.

2021

April 8, 2021 - Mercer County, PA - Undisclosed Location - Ongoing Investigation

Debbie Pregi, Bill Rigby and myself went to a previous sighting investigation site to do a followup.

Footprints have been found, as well as possible tree structures on previous investigations.

We hiked up to the bottom of a hill where we separated. I returned to my truck along with our fellow canine team member, Sinead.

Bill & Debbie continued, and they can follow up with what happened to them on a separate post along with their photos.

On my walk back, I passed several possible structures, a possible 'kill box', as well as a tall tree that caught my interest as a possible Sentinel Tree. It's in a perfect position, along multiple game trails, by a field, with views of a couple homes, and farm animals.

I found scuffs at the base which were unidentifiable to anything specific, as well as a broken tree limb from something stepping on it. There is a perfect section of the tree for something to comfortably stand or sit on for periods of time, that looks used for that purpose. Possibilities. But it is an active area. We will return to follow up.

1. 2:00am approximate - I cannot recall the date. It was either very cloudy, or during a darker end of the moon cycle: One night, I was taking my dog outside before going to bed. She was in the enclosed pen that we have outside the garage man door. I saw what I think were deer moving across the yard towards the neighbors property. Suddenly, I saw this huge (much taller than me - I'm 5'1") grey shape run across the yard and disappear into the darkness in the same direction as the deer. I assumed it was the same grey Bigfoot I had seen a few years previous on the neighbors property.

2. Same approximate time of the night as previous report - about 2:00-3:00am. The moon was brighter, but not a full moon. I was again taking the dog outside before going to bed. The enclosed dog pen is now gone, and she can run further out in the yard to do her 'business', now that she's grown out of the willful puppy stage, and willing to listen. She ran partway out, towards our garden, straight ahead. In that same direction, about 75' away is the neighbors house. He leaves his outside lights

on in front of his garage, with his pickup truck parked
there. I spotted movement, and saw what I thought was
my neighbor, standing beside the pickup truck on the
opposite side. All I could see was his shoulders and head.
He has a newer Dodge Ram 4WD. I couldn't make out
features, just I thought it was my neighbor standing
there. Afterwards, I find out that his pickup truck stands
about 6' tall. So, whatever/whomever was standing there,
was over 7' tall. Unless he was standing on a box next to
the truck.

August 3-4, 2021 - Erie National Wildlife Refuge
8/3-4/2021 PBP TEAM INVESTIGATION

Our Team (myself, Debbie Pregi, Bill Rigby, and Beth
McCandless) travelled to the witness home, and received
more information on her sighting, as well as additional
information on the area and other encounters.
We drove around the Wildlife Refuge with the witness,
stopped and geo tagged a few areas for a night time
investigation. The witness was uncertain of the exact
spot where she had taken the photo of the Bigfoot, since
it had been in 2019. We had the photos of the horses, the
field they were in and the field where the Bigfoot was to
use as reference, so we found it. Geo tagged it, and
returned to the witness home to pick up another team
member and drive back out in my truck for further
investigation. Unfortunately, the property that the
Bigfoot was on is marked Private Property by recent

signs and purple paint, so we were unable to access the exact spot. We took photos of the tree line that the Bigfoot was on, found the approximate spot where he sat and stood in the photo.
OUR FINDINGS: Possible Bigfoot

Good area, farmland containing live stock and farmlands, bordering the National Wildlife Refuge. Varied resource of Food, Water and Shelter in abundance.

Original Report:
Location: NW PA

Sept 27, 2020 approximately 1:00pm

Camera: Galaxy A21

A member privately submitted a photo to me, asking for my opinion. Shared with her permission.

The location was across a field, and her camera was on 1/4 zoom. "There's 3 big trees to the left n one behind to the right. "

Edited after clarification: She wasn't alone, was with her sister. They got spooked and left. They had taken photos of horses in a field across the road. When the horses spooked, she looked behind her. She took a photo, then 6 rapid fire photos. Then they left. She thought it was a bear.

I zoomed in to the figure in the photo. Of course, the photo pixelates so you can't make out features, but you can vaguely make out eyes.

Perhaps someone else with better photo editing skills can bring out a bit more.

I'll get up there to the location in a few weeks to do a follow up. The location is very much prime Bigfoot area, with a history of other sightings and encounters.

Edit: I added 6 additional follow up photos that the witness took immediately after the first photo. She took the photos from the drivers side window, window down, car stopped. She states her hand may have moved up or down slightly. She held her finger on the button so the camera took 6 rapid photos.

She thought it was a bear. But it was too big and the head looked different.

We investigated and was unable to get into the exact spot for a height or size comparison. Due to No Trespassing signage.

Findings: After seeing the spot, we find it to be a Possible Bigfoot

The area has ample Food, Water and Shelter resources

History of other Bigfoot activity in the area.

August 28, 2021 - Salt Fork State Park

Regretfully, due to health issues, Sinead & I had to return home from the Salt Fork State Park SOSBI Campout.
I had a great time though & plan on returning when the temperature is cooler & mosquitoes not as rabid.
This is a fantastic area, very active right in camp, with juveniles.
First day & night we had footprints right in camp, vocals, eye shine & tree knocks.
Bill Rigby & one other researcher had a sighting. A crouching Bigfoot was about 10' from Bill Rigby when they were on a night hike. He'll tell you more about his experiences when he returns.
I heard a whoop, scream, tree knock & saw eye shine at the edge of camp.

September 10-12, 2021 - Willow Bay Bradford PA Campout Sept 10-12
Bradford PA Research Trip
September 10-12
Willow Bay State Campground, Bradford PA

Friday September 10, 2021
I got into camp at 2:00 pm, set up camp and looked around the area. There was no phone or wifi available in camp, which is located in a valley. We were camped on the Aspen Loop, along Willow Creek. Wifi is only available around the campground store/office at the entrance.

From https://www.fs.usda.gov/recarea/allegheny/recreation/camping-cabins/recarea/?recid=6119&actid=101

"Willow Bay Recreation Area was built in the early 1960s by the U. S. Army Corps of Engineers. When completed, it was transferred to the USDA, Forest Service. Willow Bay Recreation Area is located 15 miles west of Bradford, PA, on State Route (SR) 346, just south of the New York State line. The area overlooks the south shore of Willow Bay, a small arm on the eastern side of the Allegheny Reservoir.
There are four camping loops - Oak, Aspen, Hemlock and Deer Grove. Campsites in Hemlock and Deer Grove Loops overlook Willow Bay while sites in Oak and Aspen loops back onto Willow Creek.
The North Country National Scenic Trail crosses near this campground and visitors can acces the trail from State Route 346."

Group Members Debbie Pregi, Paul Pelc, and David Clark attended, coming in Friday throughout the day. A couple stopped by on Saturday, who were unable to stay for that nights explorations.

Saturday September 11, 2021
Paul, Debbie and David went out to hike the area
Debbie and Paul explored the creek, finding footprints and possible tree structures. This information was given to Jason Colley, the owner/founder of East Bradford Bigfoot group, the local researcher who we were collaborating with that weekend.
After an excellent pot luck campfire dinner at Paul's cabin, we went out at 6:00pm for the evenings explorations.
We stopped at Droney first, due to the activity we previously experienced at that location in 2019. See my audio/video here: https://youtu.be/mzMmgATlkzw

On the previous trip, we experienced a power knock immediately as soon as pulled into the parking lot. During that trip various members of our group experienced rocks thrown, a thermal sighting of a tree peeker, I heard movement and along with another team member, we were bluff charged, as well as a possible young juvenile Bigfoot crawled underneath my pickup truck.
We knew the area was very active.

Debbie, Paul and David hiked out with a walkie talkie to remain in contact with me. I stayed at the parking lot with the other walkie talkie, so that I could see if there was activity on the hillside again. I heard faint rustlings, heard wood knocks, but nothing else. The team hiked back, and we sat there for awhile. Paul & David hiked on the upper trail.

They returned. We heard rustlings, wood knocks, possible vocals.

I took a video for 40 minutes while I was alone, will upload to YouTube on our Channel Pennsylvania Bigfoot Project / Monkey Wench.

Jason Colley surprised us by driving in. We heard more possible knocks and vocals.

He offered to take us to his Area X, which we were very enthusiastic to explore. I was there in 2019 and went on the hike with Jason and his assistant then.

This year, I stayed at the entrance aka Base, with a walkie talkie to stay in touch just in case.

While I was at Base, I heard vocals coming from different areas. When the team returned, they reported hearing vocals also.

I'll let Debbie, David and Paul report on their hikes.

We returned to Willow Bay after 12:30, tired but happy with the evenings adventures.

Both Debbie and Paul had camped there previously, and Paul has photos of possible prints, and structures. We'll return with a new game plan, since certain areas need a break from Bigfooting. Previously, Jason had shown me other areas to explore, so we'll put those areas, as well as a few others, on our future list.

Sunday September 12, 2021
We all packed up and headed home, tired, happy and satisfied with the short weekends explorations.   We Will Return!

10/01/21 Salt Fork State Park Scouting Trip Report
10/01/2021 Day 1
Salt Fork State Park
Cambridge, Ohio
Report:
Bill Rigby & myself
Preliminary area scout prior to Oct trip with larger group
We Drove around a bit to a few areas. That had previous reports, as well as areas that looked promising.
We found Lots of deer.
Then we went to The Group Camp where there is always activity as well as where Bill had his first sighting 5 weeks previous.
We found a stick that had been stuck into the ground. Unfortunately we didn't take a photo. We thought it was a broken off sapling in a bad spot for the campers.
We bumped it, it fell over, where we discovered that it had been jammed into the ground.
We Checked to see if it had fallen from a tree, but the tree nearby did not have broken branches.
Checking around, maintain silence to listen for movement.

Heard noises, possibly walnuts falling to the ground.
Then we spotted eye shine high up, left side of entrance
where eye shine is usually seen, at the tree line, near
where Bill saw the Bigfoot 5 weeks ago.
Thick brush where the figure was standing.
Nothing showed in that thick brush on my FLIR.
The eye shine disappeared. We moved over to check
where we had seen us and discovered a series of zig zag
trails that something large could move through.
Area: Marsh and lakes below, downhill from the
campsite approximately 500 yards away. Walking/hiking
trails at either end of camp.
Previous activity: My truck had been rocked while I slept
inside.
Something banged the side of an RV while we stood 100'
away full daylight.
During a meeting, a large figure was seen standing at a
picnic table, cooler and food there, nothing disturbed,
full daytime.
Eye shine frequently seen in one area.
Bigfoot seen peeking out at a camper, approximately 8'.
Foot prints found.
— with Bill Rigby.

We will return In a few weeks with a larger group.

Day 2 October 2, 2021 Report upcoming.

NOTE: Both Bill and I noticed photos missing from our cameras. Unknown cause. I have an Apple iPhone, Bill has an Android phone.

Some photos are from Day 2
Report upcoming.
Tree break & trackway found.

2022

March 10-15, 2022 - Land Between the Lakes Camping Trip, Kentucky - to the BEAST Meet Greet and Eat Meetup

Returned from a research trip and 'Meet & Greet' with the BEAST team at Land Between the Lakes KY.
Report: I ran my new dashcam all the way, testing it for possible night visitors by my truck.
Tuesday March 8: I got into Redd Hollow Campground at LBL about 4:00pm. Set up camp and introduced myself to the other lady, Robin, who drove in from California that was setting up her camp and also there for the BEAST Meet & Greet. I took a drive down what I thought was the road into Colson Hollow where the M&G was being held. Very rough road, with ruts dug into the road a foot deep. Turned out, that was the wrong road. The correct road down to Colson Hollow Campground was worse.
Temperatures at night were in the 20's.
Wednesday March 9: That night after everyone went to bed, something came into camp. I woke up and spoke with Robin. She had a 'visitor' to her camp overnight

who raided food that she had accidentally left on her picnic table. It lifted a can out of the box and set it on the table. It ate her candy, meat snacks for her dog, potato chip bag neatly ripped along the front, and other items. Raccoons would have gotten into her garbage bag and eaten the half sandwich inside and strewn trash all over her camp. Squirrels wouldn't have been able to lift the pop/soda can out of the box.

I hoped that with my new dash cam with night vision and motion sensor that I may have caught our 'visitor'. Unfortunately, not.

Robin and I drove down into the Colson Hollow Camp in my pickup, found the main BEAST Team already set up there. Good times sitting around the campfire with old friends.

Coonbo and Jim Osmer pulled into camp after dark. Temperatures at night were more comfortable in the low 30's.

Thursday March 10: Potluck Breakfast at Coonbo's Trailer. Included fresh Coffee, Scrambled Eggs, Bacon, Biscuits and my contribution of Home Fries. I forgot and left my Wok and lid there. Coonbo said he'd mail them back to me.

We all went down into the BEAST Camp, found the road had been repaired. Robin tore down her camp at Redd Hollow and set up at Colson Hollow. I kept my camp at Redd Hollow.

Met up with old friends from my days on the BEAST Team, gave and received much needed HUGS from all.

Later that evening, Coonbo, Jim Osmer, Jack from BigDogt2b podcast, and Greg Howse in his truck along with 7 others in another couple vehicles went out to see if we could get the Bigfoot to respond. We hit up several different areas in the park, did several calls using different techniques, got nothing but silence in reply.

I asked Coonbo what type Bigfoot there are at LBL. He told me he's only seen the Type 2 Bigfoot there. I said that's on my Bucket List to see a Type 2 Bigfoot.

The 'Boogers' didn't want to come out to play that night. We went to dinner at a Mexican restaurant with excellent food. Our party of 10 took up an entire wall of the restaurant. Good thing they were mostly empty! Temperatures at night were in the low 30's.

Friday March 11: Winter storm coming, with temperatures steady dropping into the teens.

I drove down into the Colson Hollow Camp to say goodbye to everyone. Drove back into Redd Hollow to pack up my truck, and left there about 3:00pm. I drove until 6:00pm with the roads worsening, until I got into Leitchfield KY and stayed overnight at the Hatfield Inn. I woke up to find several inches of ice and snow on the ground and covering my truck. Scraped it off and got on the road about 9:00am. The highways were mostly clear, with some snow blown onto them in places from the high winds.

2 gas fill ups coming down, filled up again once I got into the LBL area. Filled up before leaving, and filled up again somewhere in Ohio. Gasoline ranged in price from

$3.69 in Kentucky, to $3.99 to $4.09 and $4.19 in Ohio. Pennsylvania gasoline prices were at $4.39.

July 25, 2022 - The other day, a few miles away, I heard the fire siren go off in the town of Chewton. That was to my SE. To the North, just over the ridge, a pack of coyotes started yapping & going off.
I half expected to hear a Sudden sharp Yip at the end of the coyotes song, but the Bigfoot in the area didn't take advantage, or they weren't in the area.
It reminded me of the time we were in Oklahoma on an expedition, along the Red River, Deep in a forest, Texas and wilderness on the other side. We were standing by our trucks when out of nowhere, we heard what sounded like a fire truck siren. Coonbo told us, "That ain't no fire truck! There's nothing across the river for miles! That's a Booger!"
It sounded like what we know of as the Ohio Howl, an Alpha challenge call.
Only the one in Oklahoma held his longer.
In Land Between the Lakes, Tennessee side, one night, the Bigfoot put out a short call, got the coyotes yapping & singing & then a sudden sharp Yip! The next day, a couple members of our group found the mangled body of the coyote that was killed in that Bigfoot hunt. The body was literally twisted like someone wringing a wet towel. I've shown a few people on here the photo of that poor coyote. At least it was quick.

August 12-14, 2022 - PA BIGFOOT PROJECT COUNTY CHAPTER LEADS CAMPOUT REPORT: BALD EAGLE STATE PARK AUGUST 12-14

August 12: I arrived at the campground and met up with Glen Bourassa Lackawanna County Chapter Lead & AJ Grabosky Monroe & Carbon County Chapter Lead.

Our South Central PA Chapter Team: Robert Lighty Adams County Chapter Lead, Bill Furino York County Chapter Lead & Gary Fetterman teammate set up camp below below me.

Glen & AJ reported that there was a possibility that they were "paced" while exploring the area on their e-bikes. Glen stated that he heard something walking in the woods alongside them, while AJ reported hearing something walking through the woods, stepping on sticks, making noise.

Later that night, Bob, Bill, Gary and myself went to different areas, looking for activity. We heard coyotes in a few different areas.

Saturday August 13: We were invited to speak at a Bigfoot Town Hall at the Germania Hotel. We had a pretty large crowd, along with a reporter from an area newspaper who stayed for the entire 2 hours. The crowd engaged and asked numerous questions, making it a wonderful meeting!

We finally got to meet Johnathan Lackey, who volunteered to be the County Chapter Lead for Tioga County.

Bernadette Bachich Repisky Bucks County Chapter Lead and Brandon Eric McClain Bedford County

Chapter Lead were able to meet up with us at the meeting.

August 13, 2022
In Memory of Jim Hart aka 'Bubba Gump'

As some of you already know, I received an urgent phone call while we on our County Chapter Team Campout.
I received news that a Good Friend, a former Admin of the Bigfoot Outlaws Facebook Group, Admin of The Watchers group, and one of the Former Admin's of the Pennsylvania Bigfoot Project, passed away the morning of Saturday, August 13.
He had suffered another major stroke about a year and a half ago and had to leave Facebook, only coming in occasionally to read since then.
My good Friend, and Hero (oh boy, he'd scoff at that!), James Hart aka "Bubba Gump" of the Bigfoot Outlaws. You may recognize his name from a few years ago as one of our Admins, but he also co-wrote articles along with Tim "Coonbo" Baker, that I currently have in our Files section.
He and Tim grew up together, partners in crime and youthful hijinks, boogering together for many years. Best friends.
That's how I met, online, with Jim.
In 2014-15 I found the Bigfoot Outlaws, listened to them, joined their group and found that what they said

made perfect sense, and corroborated what I was learning with the Bigfoot in my area.

I wasn't alone anymore.

In January 2017, I was on the Bigfoot Crossroads podcast on their First Anniversary episode. In March, I joined them at their Land Between the Lakes, TN/KY Meet & Greet Campout. There, I met most of them in person. All but Jim Hart and Matt were there.

Jim aka 'Bear' King spoke to me there about them wanting me to become a Bigfoot Outlaw. They were going to vote on it, but he approached me first about it. Other things went on during that campout, some that I have already shared here in the group after we came home. It was an adventurous weekend, exciting and a bit confusing since my eyes were opened about the character of one of my mentors. A few months later, the Bigfoot Outlaws went through a tumultuous time, with them basically breaking apart. Some sides were taken, and my name was put out on Sasquatch Chronicles by one side. Oddly enough, mistakenly, and fortunately, VERY briefly, I was blamed for the break up. NO, I had NOTHING to do with that. The breakup was something that was brewing for many years before I even came onto the scene. I was just caught in the middle. @Jim Hart 'Bubba Gump' and Tim 'Coonbo Baker came to my rescue. Jim told me about a few things going on the inside, made me a Moderator on The Watchers group. Made me a part of his long time Team of Moderators who had been together since their days of Moderating the Bigfoot Outlaws Group.

They all became my Friends, made me feel at home. I thank them ALL for that.

Jim was outwardly gruff. 'No fucks given' was frequently bandied about. But you know, he held his feelings deeply. What a heart that man had. He loved his 'Little Man', his grandson, deeply. He'd share many photos of happy days spent with him.

Jim was hilarious, we nicknamed him 'The Dark Lord' and we were his 'Minions'. lol

He also referred to himself and Tim as 'High Tech Rednecks'. He was a computer specialist, a tech. A very intelligent man.

If you do a group search in here of his name, Jim Hart, you'll read alot of comments where he shared alot of his knowledge of Bigfoot, things he's learned and experienced. He never actually Saw a Booger, aka Bigfoot, but he's experienced much.

Tim will probably share at some point about their friendship. That is their story. I cannot tell their story. I can only talk about my Friendship with Jim.

He was featured on a Bigfoot Crossroads episode, available now, only on their archives that you need to pay to access. I hope that Matt holds it in his heart to release that particular episode back to the public on their channel. It's on their Members Only access, on Bigfoot Outlaws Radio episode 3 1 & 2, 'Sweet Home Alabama'.

I may or may not add to this post. Right now, all I can feel is a mixture of grief, love and regret that I never made enough of an effort to travel to Florence Alabama to visit and meet my Friend in Person.

August 13, 2022 - RIP - Jim "Bubba Gump" Hart
Bubba was a good friend. A hero who came to my rescue. Our Team Leader who gathered me in like a lost lamb & made me feel welcome. A no nonsense man of wisdom, intuition & integrity. He's missed, but at peace now. One day I'll get to meet him in Paradise and shake his hand.
God Bless and Thank You, Jim!

September 17, 2022 - This past weekend at the Jefferson County Bigfoot Paranormal Festival in Punxsutawney PA, an elderly gentleman and his daughter walked up to my booth. He had experienced seeing a Bigfoot on his property in Indiana County that shook him to the core. His daughter was a skeptic and unfortunately would make remarks to him that she thought was funny. This man was a highly educated man. A man retired from a university. His students would make disparaging remarks on his Facebook page. So bad, so cruel, that he was forced off of social media. This man, I could tell, suffered from PTSD. Exacerbated by the ridicule not only from his students, but also his friends and even worse, from the very people who no matter what, should support you, his own family members.

The look in this man's eyes would break anyones heart. He was beaten down. No one believed him. It broke my heart.

I tried to encourage him, let him know that I had seen Bigfoot, knew about them, told about us, my group, Pennsylvania Bigfoot Project.

THIS is why the very first Rule of the Group and the first word of our Organization motto is RESPECT. THIS is why the Second Rule is No Ridicule.

I can only pray for this man and hope that his daughter finds compassion and gives her father the love, respect and support he needs.

I can only Pray that the Ridicule ends.

The PTSD that people suffer is Real.

The Ridicule MUST end.

October 1-2, 2022 - Homewood Heritage Festival - Speaker & Vendor

We had a great time this past weekend at the Homewood Heritage Festival!

Received 3 reports, details to be shared with Brian Seech & CUE:

BIGFOOT REPORTS
  1. APRIL 2022 BIG BEAVER TWP, BEAVER COUNTY PA

BIGFOOT SEEN ON HOMEOWNERS PROPERTY, WOODED AREA. PHOTO TAKEN OF INDISCERNIBLE LARGE FIGURE STANDING

BESIDE A TREE. NO LEAVES ON THE TREES IN PHOTOS.

IF PROPERTY OWNER CONTACTS US AGAIN, WE CAN DO AN INVESTIGATION TO DETERMINE SIZE AND POSSIBILITY. OTHER REPORTS IN THE AREA.

2. MID TO LATE 1970'S NEW SEWICKLEY TWP / FREEDOM PA
LEO COUNTY SHERIFF AND FBI INVESTIGATOR CALLED TO INVESTIGATE. HE TOOK REPORT FROM THE OCCUPANTS OF TRAILER PARK. WITNESSES STATED (TO HIM) THAT A LARGE HULKING FIGURE COMING UP OUT OF A CREEK HOLLOW. OCCUPANTS OF TRAILER THOUGHT IT WAS A ANOTHER RESIDENT WHO THEY THOUGHT WAS A RETIRED WRESTLER. LEO CONTACTED THIS OTHER RESIDENT WHO DENIED BEING A WRESTLER, WAS OF LARGE GIRTH, BUT NOT HEIGHT INDICATED BY THE WITNESSES. HE ALSO SAW THE BIGFOOT AND WAS EXTREMELY FRIGHTENED. 5 TOED FOOTPRINTS FOUND. STAN GORDON CALLED TO INVESTIGATE. POLICE REPORT MYSTERIOUSLY DISAPPEARED.

1. JANUARY 2022 BEAVER COUNTY PA - PHOTOGRAPH - FOOTPRINT FOUND ON FRONT PORCH APPROXIMATELY 14" LONG. WITNESS

PUT HER FOOT BESIDE THE FOOTPRINT IN THE
SNOW TO COMPARE. WITNESS WEARS A
WOMENS SIZE 8 SHOE. FOOTPRINT
APPROXIMATELY ANOTHER 4-5" LONGER.
WITNESS ALSO STATES OTHER VOCALS HEARD
IN THE AREA.
PHOTOGRAPH SHOWN TO PBP INVESTIGATOR
MARY FABIAN. DETERMINATION: POSSIBLE
BIGFOOT PRINT.

**September 8-10, 2022 - SALT FORK STATE PARK,
OHIO**
OHIO BIGFOOT RESEARCH PROJECT &
PENNSYLVANIA BIGFOOT PROJECT GROUP
CAMPOUT
SEPTEMBER 8
Night
APPROXIMATE 10:00pm
MIKE HARTMAN, BILL RIGBY, JOSH ENDSLEY
BARB & DON STROCK ELIZABETH NEAPOLITAN
AMIE COPLAN AND MYSELF WERE SITTING
AROUND THE CAMPFIRE AT THE FRONT V OF
THE GROUP CAMP
JOSH HAD SET UP TRAIL CAMS INSIDE THE
WOOD LINE AROUND THE CAMP INCLUDING AT
THE BACK END OF CAMP
WHILE SITTING AT THE CAMPFIRE I WAS
FACING THE BACK OF THE CAMPGROUND
WHERE ACTIVITY USUALLY COMES FROM

JOSH AND MYSELF OBSERVED EYE SHINE AND
OCCASIONAL FLASH FROM THE CAM
THE EYE SHINE VARIED IN HEIGHT FROM LOW
TO GROUND TO MID HEIGHT TO 8' approximately
JOSH WALKED BACK TO THE CAM AREA AND
REPORTED HEARING A VOICE
I WENT TO BED AROUND 11:30
I WOKE UP OCCASIONALLY THROUGH THE
NIGHT STARTLED BY UNKNOWN
AT ONE POINT I HEARD A LARGE TREE BREAK
TIMES UNKNOWN
I WOKE UP AT 4:45AM
OTHERS REPORTED WAKING TO VOCALS
INCLUDING SCREAMING 1:00-1:30 FROM THE
FOOD PLOT AREA, OHIO HOWL 3:00 AM, TREE
BREAK (TIME UNKNOWN) BEHIND MY TENT &
BIPEDAL FOOTSTEPS (2-3:00AM).
I HEARD SOMETHING LIFT THE CORNER OF THE
TARP COVERING THE STOVE ON THE TABLE IN
FRONT OF MY TENT
ELIZABETH HAD HER RECORDER GOING
IT CAUGHT: TAPPING & SOMETHING
BREATHING

SEPTEMBER 9
NIGHT
AFTER THE PODCAST HOSTED BY Mike Hartman
WE SAT AROUND THE CAMPFIRE AND TALKED A
BIT. I WAS SITTING FACING THE REAR OF THE

CAMPGROUND WATCHING FOR MOVEMENT OR
EYESHINE
I SPOTTED MOVEMENT TO OUR SE INSIDE THE
TREELINE. A FEW OF THE GUYS WENT IN TO
INVESTIGATE
LATER, MYSELF, PAUL PELC, and 2 OTHERS
DROVE OUT INTO THE PARK.
WE FIRST WENT TO THE HANDICAP PICNIC
AREA.
WE PULLED IN, AND ALL WALKED TOWARDS
THE PAVILION. AS WE GOT CLOSE, WE HEARD A
LOUD BANG AS IF SOMEONE CLOSED A DOOR
VIOLENTLY ON THE OPPOSITE SIDE OF THE
PAVILION.
THE OTHER 2, GRANDMOTHER & 10 YEAR OLD
GRANDDAUGHTER STAYED BACK. PAUL WAS IN
THE LEAD, I WAS BEHIND HIM. WE STEPPED
TOWARD WHERE THE NOISE CAME FROM,
ASKING "IS SOMEONE HERE?". NO ANSWER,
BUT AS WE GOT CLOSER WE HEARD AN
INDECIPHERABLE MUMBLING CONVERSATION
THAT STOPPED AS WE GOT CLOSE.
PAUL PULLED HIS FIREARM, AND WE WALKED
CLOSER, LOOKING BETWEEN THE SLATS,
TRYING TO FIND WHO WAS THERE. WE
CHECKED BOTH BATHROOMS AND BEHIND THE
PAVILION, ON THE ROOF, NO ONE THERE.
NOTHING ELSE HAPPENED THERE.

WE DROVE FROM THERE TO THE LAKE. PAUL
DID A CALL WHICH RECEIVED A REPLY IN THE
DISTANCE.
NOTHING ELSE FOR THE NIGHT
I LEFT THE FOLLOWING DAY.

October 16-22, 2022 10/16/2022
10/16/2022 - OKLAHOMA RESEARCH TRIP
ARRIVAL
INITIAL PHOTOS & VIDEO TAKEN AT THE CABIN
More photos and Video upcoming from my Nikon P900
camera. Will post after downloading.
OKLAHOMA RESEARCH TRIP UPDATE
October 17
There is activity around camp, and one member wasn't
feeling well so we just stayed in camp all day. Rocks
thrown at the cabin, one hit the grill near where I was
standing. Not steadily thrown, just one every few hours,
enough to get a reaction from whoever was nearby.
Nothing caught on audio recorders yet.
Glen Bourassa & his cousin had to run back to OKC.
Soon after they pulled off the property, the doorbell rang.
I went to the front door & looked out, no one there. The
cabin owner has motion sensor surveillance cameras
around the cabin because of thieves (and Bigfoot), so
we'll contact him later today when we're in an area with
signal, see if anything shows up on the camera. He
caught the young female on camera running across the
yard when he first set up, but nothing since.

UPDATE ON THE DOORBELL: The property owner has a sensor at the gate to ring & notify when a vehicle passes through. That was the 'doorbell' ringing, after Glen and his cousin, Stuart drove through.
10/19/2022
OKLAHOMA RESEARCH TRIP
A member alerted me to a possible Bigfoot in a photo I had taken
Lots of things going on today, including meeting the author of "Relics", John Vandeventer, and purchasing 3 of his books.
We stopped at the Honobia Country Store & got a Bigfoot Burger & a few souvenirs.
We then drove to Talahini & visited the Bigfoot Museum.
This evening we plan on a night investigation. Separate report.
10/19/2022
OKLAHOMA RESEARCH TRIP
LOCATION: BEECH CREEK NATIONAL SCENIC BOTANICAL AREA
We had a report of an extremely large structure in this area. We drove in, immediately found numerous structures.
10/19/2022
OKLAHOMA RESEARCH TRIP
INVESTIGATION OF THE PHOTO ANOMALY AT THE CABIN
TJ Seaman spotted a possible figure in one of my random photos taken on 10/18/2022. Chuck & I

investigated and did comparison shots. There was no stump, no tree, no rock in that spot to account for the figure.

At the spot where the figure was is the top of the ravine, a cliff edge where it laid, peeking at me as I took photos. I laid pine cones and an interesting rock on top of a flat stone nearby where it laid. I'll check there this morning to see if there was any change.

DETERMINATION: Possible Bigfoot

Possibly the female that has been setn here at the cabin previously.

UPDATE: After reviewing the photo, There are 2 figures in my Oklahoma photo!

**And to let those who didn't read my original report, yes, Chuck Schlabs & I did a comparison. We checked the following day, found the exact angle and spot. We both went down. There is a bluff there that the figures were laying and peeking up over at me while I took photos of the area around the cabin. There are no stumps, trees or rocks there that the figures could be mistaken.

10/19/2022

OKLAHOMA RESEARCH TRIP

A member alerted me to a possible Bigfoot in a photo I had taken

Lots of things going on today, including meeting the author of "Relics", John Vandeventer, and purchasing 3 of his books.

We stopped at the Honobia Country Store & got a Bigfoot Burger & a few souvenirs.

We then drove to Talahini & visited the Bigfoot Museum.
This evening we plan on a night investigation.
Separate report.

10/19/2022
HONOBIA OKLAHOMA RESEARCH TRIP
DAY 4
I decided to give the female Bigfoot a name. Clementine came to mind.
Sean, the cabin owner, for some reason found that amusing. Lol I like it. Sweet Clemantine.
10/20/2022 12:47 EARLY AM DAY 5
OKLAHOMA RESEARCH TRIP
NIGHT INVESTIGATION
We set out recorders to catch possible vocals, and possibly footsteps. Previously the female Bigfoot and another have been heard walking up on the porches late at night.
I heard possible vocals, but will need to review audio.
Possible rock thrown at the cabin 12:47am.
We had planned an extensive night investigation at the cabin & surrounding.
I had 2 thermals, walkie talkies, & an audio recorder ready, Chuck had 4 recorders & night vision. We planned on hitting the area around the cabin pretty hard late night.

An emergency came up & transportation arrangements were changed. We had to pack all gear up & leave the cabin the morning of Oct 20.

An audio recorder was set out, which hopefully caught the activity we had at the cabin. We had pretty much figured that the Bigfoot would feel comfortable enough with us to come in that night, and they did.

Starting at 12:47 am, rock thrown at the cabin. We were all in bed but it woke us up.

2:00am Heavy Footsteps heard coming onto the front porch. Something turned the doorknob. Something came up onto the back porch. All blinds were closed. We had left them open late for the previous couple of nights.

2:30am (approximately) Vocals heard in the nearby woods.

We'll follow up after all audio is reviewed.

10/20/22 11:00am We were all packed up & ready to leave for Oklahoma City.

Before pulling out, I waved & said "Goodbye Clementine!"

We dropped Chuck Schlabs off at his truck at 4:30 & Deborah Kay Parker-Mcgee & I began the long trip back home, a day early.

We stopped at Claremore OK where we spent the night.

10/21/22 Sean, the cabin owner, and his girlfriend went up there on Friday. When he went out to turn everything on…..a horrible stench appeared on the scene. He said that it smelled slinky, musty, urine, fecees....really rank!!! Didn't see it but it was close by. As soon as they got into the cabin, rocks were being thrown at it. Had activity for the weekend.

November 7, 2022 Two different coyote packs were out running up and down the valley last night, singing, yipping & vocalizing like crazy. One pack to the SW were moving around quite a bit. One voice, deeper than the others started them off, kept egging them on when they'd quit calling, moving from SW to SE, until I could no longer hear them.
The pack to the NE had a deeper voiced individual start then off. They sang for a bit but ended suddenly.
I usually hear the Bigfoot hunting coyotes in the early Spring. This was unusual to hear a possible hunt in the Fall.

Our Adventure continues, as long as I am able.
I just celebrated my 67th birthday, am no longer able to hike and climb like I used to, so I go where I can, and research to the best of my abilities in ways that I can handle.

My Personal Motto is: "Life is an Adventure. Live it!"
I intend to.

I'll update this as time goes on and I find more. I've got photos in the Group Photo Album section of prints and tree structures. I should try to get the all organized into one Album File.

More trips are planned, some along with other research groups.
Please consider donating to assist in our research efforts.

Paypal.Me/MFabianPBP or Ko-Fi.com/ PennsylvaniaBigfootProject

I own and run Pennsylvania Bigfoot Project Facebook group, to learn more and share encounters. I also do audio analysis for other groups, have appeared on the Bigfoot Outlaws podcast of their First Anniversary show. I teach others against the dangers of habituation aka feeding the Bigfoot, and assist when others are having problems with them at their homes. I've traveled to Land Between the Lakes in Kentucky to do some research, and hope to travel to other areas. I have a YouTube channel under my Pennsylvania Bigfoot Project name chronicling some of my research, also.

**The Official Motto of Pennsylvania Bigfoot
Project
"Respect, Help, Share Knowledge, Learn
More & Have Fun"**

PENNSYLVANIA BIGFOOT PROJECT LOGO

THE END

My Bigfoot Family
Footprint Found North Sewickley Twp PA 2015
Footprint Oklahoma Expedition 2018

A Group Member Spotted Something in the Circled Area of the Photo

at the top of the Bluff October 2022 Honobia Ok

Caption

Zhina

Footprint - Greene County PA Investigation

My Son, Michael Barton, & Myself Playing
with a Monkey in a Park 1980

Sinead

Footprint North Sewickley Twp, Beaver County PA

Quebec Run Fayette County Investigation

Bob Gimlin & Mary Fabian

Footprint Found in North Sewickley Twp, Beaver
County PA 2015

Structure Found Shenango Twp, Lawrence County PA 2016

Structure Found Shenango Twp, Lawrence County PA 2017

Caption

Myself, drawn by Artist David Burton in
2002 for a Magazine Article on the Book
Series "Pellucidar" by Edgar Rice
Burroughs

Chuck Schlabs, Mary Fabian, Tim Baker, & Dee Doss at Brown Springs, Oklahoma 2018

17" Foot print cast from Jefferson County PA Investigation 2017

Creekfoot Campout 2018

Zhina helping me on an Investigation, North Sewickley Twp, Beaver
County PA 2014

PENNSYLVANIA BIGFOOT PROJECT GROUP CAMPOUT BRADFORD
PA 2019

Tree Break in Active Area, Near Sighting Area, X Structure and Bend,
Union Twp, Lawrence County PA 2019

Footprint After Sighting Report, Greene County PA Investigation Gas Well Trucker Films Bigfoot *See Video on our channel, Pennsylvania Bigfoot Project

TBT - My dad, Roy E. Parker aka Parker the Magician See More

Parker the Magician

Footprint Found Behind My Tent Coshocton County Ohio 2019

My Truck Bed Camping Set Up - Full Pull Out Drawer for Food & Gear
2020 Ford F150

Winter Camping Salt Fork State Park, Cambridge Ohio 2021

Night Time Investigation Quebec Run, Forbes State Forest, Fayette County PA 2021

Forbes State Forest, Fayette County PA

Caption

Coshocton County Ohio Investigation 2021 - A Fellow Researcher
Checks Out A Suspicious Noise

Photos from our Honobia Oklahoma Expedition October 2022

A Possible Baby Bigfoot in the Fork of the Tree, Moraine State Park,
Butler County PA Investigation 2016

Thank You!

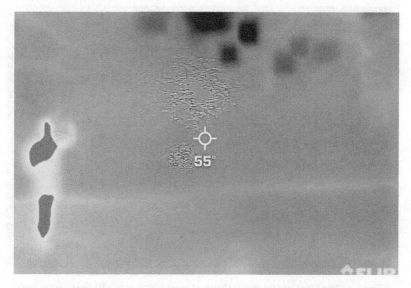

Bill Rigby and Myself Night Investigation, Salt Fork State Park Ohio 2021 - Figure Spotted in the Tree Line That the FLIR didn't pick up

Zhina at her Post at the Back Door of our Home in North Sewickley Twp, Beaver County PA. 2015 Ever Watchful for the Bigfoot

Sinead

Jefferson County Bigfoot Paranormal Expo, One of the Festivals We
Attended Punxsutawney PA 2022

At the Cabin, Honobia Oklahoma October 2022

Zoomed into that Circled Area - You can see something is there

Handprints Found on the Side of My Pickup the Morning After Something
Shook My Truck While I Slept Inside 2018

At the top of the bluff

Caption

My Husband, Lou & I

Knuckle Print in the Sand, Oklahoma 2018

Coonbo & Dave Counts Finding Footprints - Land Between the Lakes KY 2017

Footprints Found in the Grass - Salt Fork State Park Ohio 2021

Made in United States
Orlando, FL
28 July 2024

49627693R00117